Adult Instruction in the Catholic Faith

Renewal of Faith

Rev. Thomas White
and
Desmond O'Donnell, O.M.I.

Ave Maria Press / Notre Dame / Indiana 46556

First printing, April 1974
Second printing, June 1975
45,000 copies in print

Nihil Obstat: T. Veech, D.Sac.Hist., Censor Deputatus
Imprimatur: James Madden, V.G., Sydney

Originally published in serial form by The Catholic Enquiry Centre of Australia

Library of Congress Catalog Card Number: 74-76320
International Standard Book Number: 0-87793-068-6

Printed in the United States of America

Renewal of Faith

Contents

About This Book

Renewal of Faith is a basic approach to the Catholic religion designed to renew personal faith in Jesus Christ and commitment to the Church as the Christian community. It is meant to lead both individuals and groups to a new religious experience on the basis of openness to the Spirit and acceptance of Jesus Christ as the cornerstone of the Christian faith.

It is suggested that the book be not merely read but prayerfully studied by all who want to understand and integrate into their lives the new emphasis on coresponsibility, dialogue, community, scripture, and the Holy Spirit in the Church today. It incorporates in its approach and method the spiritually enriching direction of Vatican II.

The format of *Renewal of Faith* is educational, not merely informational. It is meant to be an experience which leads to a committed Christian life. Scripture is a necessary and considerable part of the program. So is prayer, which is suggested at appropriate points. The scripture, the prayer, and the discussion points at the end of each chapter are designed to bring Christian thinking and action into line with the word of God.

Chapter 1

JESUS IS LORD

A Changing World

(1)   The world we live in is constantly changing as man with the wonderful creative abilities placed within him by God continually searches for and finds something new. Man first farmed with stone implements but later discovered steel. He was once a blacksmith but then became an engineer. Train travel became possible by the discovery of steam power and now anyone who wants to, can travel beyond the speed of sound and a few can visit the moon. This is the world into which God placed us—a world which never lets us put aside our faculty of wonder, because of its never-ending possibilities for showing us something we hardly thought about before.

(2)   When we become accustomed to change it is often very beneficial and enjoyable, but change can come so quickly that it makes us uncomfortable. Books are now being written about "future shock" describing how difficult it is for us to adapt to rapid change in the world around us. One book simply tries to answer the question: "Can we survive our future?" It points out that things are getting faster and faster and when this happens most of us feel a

little frightened even if we do hope for better things sooner.
In short, it is normal to feel a slight confusion and insecurity
when presented with change, especially in things which we
might have thought almost unchangeable.

(3)   But change usually has the effect of making us look
        more deeply at what we possess. When a building we
live in shows cracks, we have a look at the foundations.
When a new supersonic jet costs some millions, people
usually ask "Do we need it?" So even if change is not always
a good thing, it has this value that it makes us think again
about what should or should not change. While God has
made man creative, he has also put into him the urge to ask
if what is changing is good for him.

Change in the Church

(4)   Is the Church part of this changing world? Is the
        Church changing? The Church is part of this world
because we are the Church. Yet in another way it is not
part of the world because it contains realities which are
unchanging and unchangeable as God himself. The change-
able part of the Church is certainly changing and even
though we know this does not mean change in any of the
fundamentals, it naturally makes us—like all change does
—a little nervous, uncomfortable and feel threatened. This
is natural enough.

(5)   As with any change it has the advantage that it makes
        us look more deeply at what cannot change. It makes
us look at our fundamentals once again. We know that
many people today are asking such sensible questions as:
"Is everything changing?" "Is nothing the same?" "What
next in the Church?" This reaction is a good one provided

you pursue the question rather than panic before you have heard the answer. You, reading this book, are among those who sensibly seek the answer.

Why This Book?

(6)   We have written this book not merely to explain that none of the important things in the Church is changing, but primarily to help you look at the important things in your life. We know that you have already learned about your faith and the teaching of the Church. So, this is not a book telling you what you already know; in fact, it presumes that you know what every Catholic, young and old, knows pretty well. We mean such fundamental facts as God's existence, and everything contained in the Creed which we say together at Mass. These chapters are written not merely to make you feel safe in a changing Church, but to help you deepen your faith and benefit from the changes which are good. It will also help you to reject the changes which are not good.

(7)   It is presumed here that if you did not already love God and if you were not trying sincerely to live a good Christian life, you would not have opened this book. Therefore, our first aim in offering it to you is to help you deepen your Catholic faith and gain more and more from those things which can never change in that faith revealed by Jesus to his apostles and now taught by his Church through the guidance of the Holy Spirit. So, the purpose of the book is a very positive one, namely to help you to grow in the faith, hope and love given you by God's goodness at your baptism and strengthened again at your confirmation. By achieving this, we at the same time will help you not to worry about changes which are taking place.

(8)   In offering this book, our purpose is best expressed
in St. Paul's prayer for the Christians at Ephesus:

*This, then is what I pray, kneeling before the Father,
from whom every family, whether spiritual or natural,
takes its name. Out of his infinite glory, may he give you
the power through his Spirit for your hidden self to
grow strong, so that Christ may live in your hearts
through faith, and then, planted in love and built on
love, you will with all the saints have the strength to
grasp the breadth, and the length, the height and the
depth; until knowing the love of Christ, which is beyond
all knowledge, you are filled with the utter fullness of
God.*

*Glory be to him whose power, working in us, can do
infinitely more than we can ask or imagine; glory be to
him from generation to generation in the Church and in
Christ Jesus for ever and ever. Amen.* (Eph. 3: 14-21)

Your Personal Attitude

(9)   Your approach to this subject is important because
what we offer is not just information about theology or
even religion; it is God's word to inspire you and deepen
your faith. Consequently, it will be important to listen with
the ears of your heart. The book will be of real value to you
only if you ask the Holy Spirit to fill your heart as you
study it. Jesus told us that God has hidden the important
things from those who are "learned and clever" and that he
reveals them to those who have a simple and childlike attitude before him (Mt 11:25). In fact, he has told us clearly
that unless we approach God with the simplicity and humility of a little child we will never get to heaven. In other
words, your approach must be one of prayer more than

one of analysis. At the same time you must be very confident tnat nothing we say will be beyond your understanding if your heart is humbly searching for God's word.

(10) May we suggest that you spend some time right now praying the thoughts contained in these words of Sacred Scripture. Take them very slowly:

> *May the God of our Lord Jesus Christ the*
> *Father of glory, give me*
> *—a spirit of wisdom and perception of*
> *what is revealed, to bring me*
> *—to full knowledge of him.*
> *May he enlighten the eyes of my mind so that I can see*
> *—what hope his call holds for me,*
> *what riches he has promised I will inherit (and)*
> *—how infinitely great is the power he has exercised*
> *for me.* (cf. Eph 1:17-19)

Is Everything Changing?

(11) Some people ask today if everything in our religion is changing. God himself gives us the answer. We can be very sure of it because it *is* God's answer.

> *Jesus Christ is the same today as he was yesterday and he will be the same for ever.* (Heb 13:8)

It is for this reason that the next sentence tells us:

> *Do not let yourselves be led astray by all sorts of strange doctrines.* (Heb 13:9)

(12) Everything is measured and assessed by these assurances of God to us his people. If our faith in Jesus is deep then we cannot be led astray by "strange doctrines."

The Spirit of Jesus will guide our hearts enabling us to remain firm on him and to recognize what is not from him. He has never changed, will never and can never change; he is permanently "the Way, the Truth and the Life" (Jn 14:6). Jesus does not change and so everything is not changing. Some things will be the same forever. While we accept changes in the world and in the Church, we must never be led astray from "the shepherd and guardian of our souls" (1 Pt 2:25).

(13) This book is about him — Jesus who is the same today as he was yesterday and who will be the same forever — on whom we all have built our faith. We can rejoice in this unchanging certainty in our lives.

The Word, who is life —
this is our subject. (1 Jn 1:1b)

Let us approach it confidently, humbly and prayerfully together.

No Other Foundation
(14) St. Paul heard that the Christians at Corinth were confused with many new ideas and that they were divided in their allegiance to different leaders in the Church. So he recalled this fundamental fact to them:

By the grace God gave me, I succeeded as an architect and laid the foundations, on which someone else is doing the building. Everyone doing the building must work carefully. For the foundation, nobody can lay any other than the one which has already been laid, that is Jesus Christ. (1 Cor 3:10-11)

(15) Everything you accept in being a Catholic is based on this foundation; there can be no other. This is the Jesus who founded the Church; who guides that Church; the Jesus who chose Mary as his mother; the Jesus who gave us his body in the Eucharist; the Jesus whose passion, death and resurrection we proclaim on our altars at Mass. It is the same Jesus who forgives us our sins when we confess them, having given that power to his Church; this is the Jesus who died, is risen and will come again, who by dying destroyed our death and by rising restored our life, who by his cross and resurrection has set us free and is now the savior of the world, as we say after the consecration at Mass.

(16) It is faith in him and on him that makes us what we are, members of his Church and

a chosen race, a royal priesthood, a consecrated nation, a people set apart to sing the praises of God who called you out of darkness into his wonderful light.
(1 Pt 2:9)

No change can alter this. Any change which does alter it cannot be in the will of God. It is on this faith in the unchanging Jesus Christ that your life is based. Against it you can examine and evaluate any change in the Church. If the change helps people to deepen or express their faith in Jesus then it is good; if not it cannot be from God. Everything must be founded and built on faith in Jesus as the Lord. Here is how St. Jude wrote about it to the first Christians:

But you, my dear friends, must use your most holy faith as your foundation and build on that, praying in the Holy Spirit. (Jude 1:20)

Change Has Its Dangers

(17) Not all change is good. We cannot be guided by what the latest theologian thinks even though he may be very skilled in theology. The Church is not a group of people led by experts; it is the people of God led by the Good Shepherd, Jesus Christ, and those whom he has appointed. Today we have many sheep experts but we must remind ourselves that there is only one shepherd.

I am the good shepherd;
I know my own,
and my own know me . . .
They too will listen to my voice. (Jn 10:14, 16)

Jesus is "the shepherd and guardian of your souls" (1 Pt 2:25).

(18) Our natural hesitance about changes in the Church is a good thing especially if we are concerned lest something important is being lost or neglected. Even in the early Church Peter found it necessary to say this (he was talking about misusing Sacred Scripture):

Be careful not to get carried away by the errors of un-
principled people, from the firm ground that you are
standing on. Instead, go on growing in the grace and
in the knowledge of our Lord and savior Jesus Christ.
(2 Pt 3:17-18)

At the same time, let us remind ourselves that no serious errors can come from the Church to which Jesus has promised:

Know that I am with you always; yes, to the end of time.
(Mt 28:20)

Speaking about the Church as the body of Christ, St. Paul stresses that we have one body, one Spirit, one Lord, one faith, one baptism and one God who is Father of all and so he assures us:

> *Then we shall not be . . . tossed one way and another and carried along by every wind of doctrine, at the mercy of all the tricks men play and their cleverness in practicing deceit.* (Eph 4:14)

Your Own Foundations

(19) Before we look more deeply at Jesus as the foundation of our faith it is well for each one of us to look carefully at our own Christian foundations. Although we are members of the Church and presumably good ones; it may be that some practices or persons, some duties or devotions, good in themselves, have become disconnected from the source which was their origin. This is a matter of self-examination for each of us. Because one of your favorite prayers is no longer said in public, or because the priest in the pulpit uses "with-it" words rather than the ones you are accustomed to, you may be a little worried. Or when a priest you know well asks for a dispensation from his priesthood, or when the new priest encourages the youngsters to sing their prayers the way they like best, you may feel more than uncomfortable.

(20) If you feel not only a little uncomfortable but are annoyed to the extent of anxiety it may be that you have been putting too much emphasis on this prayer, that hymn, a particular law or an individual priest. You may find that you have allowed some person, prayer or religious practice to receive too much importance compared with the

place due to Jesus as the foundation of your life. Should
this be so we can only ask that you listen carefully to the
words of Jesus which we offer you in this book and you
will then know that:

*Therefore, everyone who listens to these words of mine
and acts on them will be like a sensible man who built
his house on a rock. Rain came down, floods rose, gales
blew and hurled themselves against that house, and it
did not fall: it was founded on a rock.* (Mt 7:24-25)

(21) Through no fault of your own, your education in the
        faith may have stopped when formal schooling did.
You may have developed in every other aspect of your
personality but not in this. This book will remedy this by
helping you to achieve a more adult grasp of your faith. It
can be a starting point for a whole new look at your faith
and a renewed living of it.

Fundamental Questions About Jesus

(22) Realizing the importance of a question is just as im-
        portant as finding the answer. This is especially true
of questions about Jesus. The more deeply we accept the
questions, the more deeply we give the answer. It is something we must pray about rather than just think about, a
question we must ask in our hearts, not just in our heads.
Any question about Jesus is addressed from the Holy Spirit
directly to our spirit which is the deepest part of us. We all
need to pray that we will hear the questions with all that
they imply.

(23) The way we answer can be very deep or very shallow
        or just in between. But on the depth of our answer will

depend the quality of our faith and our stability in our faith in these times of change. The answers to these questions must be given differently from answers to any other questions in life. There are two reasons for this.

(24) Firstly, the answer is going to affect my whole life. The kind of answer I give will be a thermometer of my Christian life. As with the question, the answer must involve me totally; it must take over my whole life, and in all its aspects. That is why once I become an adult, no one else can answer it for me even if others tell me the answer they have found. My answer must be my own.

(25) Secondly, unlike any other answer to any other question, my finding it depends on a direct gift from God. I cannot find it myself even if I use the right words which sound like the right answer. All I can do is to provide a humble ready-to-listen heart while God gives me the answer. God must reveal it to me if it is to get beyond my lips as words and deeper than my head as theory. When St. Peter gave his answer, Jesus said:

> *You are a happy man! Because it was not flesh and blood that revealed this to you but my Father in heaven.* (Mt 16:17)

Jesus Said: "Who Do You Say I Am?"

(26) Who do we believe that Jesus is? This is the most important question in history; it is also the central question of every Christian. Jesus was a Palestinian carpenter who lived and died in a very small corner of the world. He offered many signs and wonders to show that he was more than merely man, he claimed equality with God. God supported his claim by the supreme sign of his resurrection

from death. Here is how St. Peter put it to his countrymen:

God made this Jesus whom you crucified both Lord and Christ. (Acts 2:36)

i.e., God has testified to Christ's divinity and to the fact that he is the appointed redeemer. Our faith in this must be total. Do you believe without any reservations that Jesus is the Lord, that he is God? St. John gives us a unique statement of Jesus' divinity:

(27)
In the beginning was the Word:
the Word was with God
and the Word was God . . .
The Word was made flesh,
and he lived among us,
and we saw his glory,
the glory that is his as the only Son of the Father
full of grace and truth. (Jn 1:1,14)

(28) Our entire life as Christians depends on the truth contained in these words. Do you really believe that the Palestinian carpenter called Jesus is truly the Son of God, equal to God the Father?

In his own words to those who questioned him:

I tell you most solemnly before Abraham was I AM.
(Jn 8:58)

(29) Are you really prepared to accept this direct claim of Jesus to be God? Or more practically are you ready to accept it so deeply that it will affect your entire life?

It is not difficult to say in the Creed at Mass:

We believe in one Lord, Jesus Christ,
the only Son of God,
eternally begotten of the Father,
God from God, Light from Light,
true God from true God
. . . born of the Virgin Mary and became man . . .
On the third day he rose again in fulfillment of
the scriptures.

(30) You can accept this in the sense that you say it with
your voice and don't disbelieve it. You can think it in
your mind and agree with it in an uninvolved sort of way
without having it affect your life. Or you can give full and
very deep assent to it so that it brings about a complete
change in your life. Only when you have given full and
deep assent to it will you have accepted Jesus' claim to be
God. When he made his claim and asked for a response,
some walked away, some scorned him as being a devil,
others crucified him. A few heard the claim deep in their
hearts and said as St. Peter did:

You are the Christ, the Son of the living God. (Mt
16:16)

(31) At this point in this first chapter we suggest that you
pray for the grace to hear this question deeply and
hear Jesus ask you from his Sacred Heart:

But you, who do YOU say I am? (Mt 16:15)

What is your answer? Your very personal answer? Speak
to him, tell him now.

Jesus Came to Give Life

(32) Our next basic question is: "Why has Jesus come?"
or "What does he offer us?" This is a question which
you should not be afraid to ask and think about prayerfully
very often. As a well-instructed Catholic, you probably
have known the answer in a general way since childhood.
But we suggest that you rediscover the question now as an
adult and then give a freer and fuller answer than you gave
as a child.

(33) Jesus tells us that he came so that we might have
"eternal life":

I have come
so that they may have life
and have it to the full. (Jn 10:10)

(34) And what is this life?

Eternal life is this:
to know you,
the only true God,
and Jesus Christ whom you have sent. (Jn 17:3)

Before fully accepting what Jesus has to offer, we need to
receive from God the power to understand and appreciate
the gift that is offered to us.

(35) In Jesus, God became our personal Savior

our great God and savior Christ Jesus (Ti 2:14)

to bring us out of the sinful state in which all mankind is
born. This we call salvation or redemption or righteousness.

(36) He now appears

in the actual presence of God on our behalf (Heb 9:24)

making us acceptable to God through the merits of his death. The Father showed that he accepted that death when he called his Son from the tomb on Easter Sunday morning.

Brothers and Sisters of Jesus

(37) On that morning Jesus appeared to Mary Magdalen and proclaimed that through his victory over sin and death, men could now become his brothers and call God their Father.

Go and find my brothers, and tell them:
I am ascending to my Father and to your Father,
to my God and your God. (Jn 20:17)

(38) Think well on this great privilege — God is in truth your Father — about which the author of the letter to the Hebrews wrote:

For the one who sanctifies, and the ones who are sancti-
fied, are of the same stock; that is why he openly calls
them brothers. (Heb 2:11)

Together with the Spirit of Jesus which dwells in you now, acknowledge this great gift by saying the "Our Father" slowly . . .

Jesus Is the Way and the Truth

(39) Jesus also offers us someone we can imitate and a teaching we can follow — a way and a truth — in his own person. But the supreme gift of God to us in Jesus is his Holy Spirit of whom we shall speak in another chapter. And all this for no other reason than God's great love for us:

We were still helpless when at his appointed moment
Christ died for sinful men. It is not easy to die even
for a good man—though of course for someone really
worthy, a man might be prepared to die—but what
proves that God loves us is that Christ died for us while
we were sinners . . . we are filled with joyful trust
in God, through our Lord Jesus Christ, through whom
we have already gained our reconciliation. (Rom
5:7,11)

(40) St. John who knew the love of Christ so closely reminds us:

Yes, God loved the world so much that he gave his only
son, so that everyone who believes in him may not be
lost but may have eternal life. (Jn 3:16)

(41) In the words of Jesus himself:

As the Father has loved me so I have loved you. (Jn
15:9)

I have loved them as much as you loved me. (Jn 17:23)

Jesus Is Everything

(42) When St. Paul wrote to the newly converted Christians
in Colossae he told them:

There is only one Christ; he is everything and he is in
everything. (Col 3:11)

When we can say this more deeply every day, we are
growing in faith.

(43) When we begin to recognize the importance of the
two questions we asked earlier in this lesson our faith

has begun to grow. St. Paul did not meet Christ until he was an adult but because he fully accepted Jesus as "Lord and Christ," as his God and Savior, he was able to write to the Christians at Galatia:

I live now not with my own life but with the life of Christ who lives in me. The life I now live in this body I live in faith: faith in the Son of God who loved me and who sacrificed himself for my sake. (Gal 2:20)

What Does Jesus Ask of Me?

(44) He asks three things:

Repent.

Believe.

Receive the Holy Spirit.

We shall consider these in the next chapters.

POINTS FOR DISCUSSION

1. List some of the things in our religion which you feel can never change.

2. Why did Vatican II make so many changes?

3. What would you consider to be the foundation on which our religion rests?

4. What is your personal answer to the question: "Who do you believe Jesus is?"

REVIEW

Before attempting this review it is important that you read and study the chapter carefully. Unless you do this the educational value of the book will be lost for you.

In this review you will find a number of statements each of which is either true or false. Read each one and *draw a circle* around the letter which indicates your answer — T or F — after each statement.

1. The speed of change in the world is continually increasing.   T   F

2. Change that is too rapid leads usually to some confusion and insecurity.   T   F

3. Man usually accepts change without question.   T   F

4. God's Church cannot change in any way.   T   F

5. The purpose of this book is just to explain changes in the Church.   T   F

6. Change in the Church can be either good or bad.   T   F

7. The purpose of this book is to help you teach religion better.   T   F

8. This is a book on modern theology.   T   F

9. The more intelligent one is the more benefit one will get from this book.   T   F

10. Unless one prays while reading this book, little will be gained.   T   F

11. Anything in the Church can eventually
    change.   T   F

12. Theologians are the best guides to
    God's truth.   T   F

13. The pope is the foundation of our
    faith.   T   F

14. Faith in Jesus makes us members of
    his Church.   T   F

15. A natural hesitance about change in
    the Church is good.   T   F

16. The religious education of most people
    stops after school.   T   F

17. My answer to "Who is Jesus?" will
    affect my whole life.   T   F

18. My answer to "Who is Jesus?" can be
    found in good books.   T   F

19. My faith in Jesus as Lord can be deep,
    shallow or in between.   T   F

20. If I can say the Creed, I really have
    faith.   T   F

21. Jesus came on earth merely to preach
    about God.   T   F

22. Jesus offers us the power to call God
    our Father.   T   F

23. If one does not accept Jesus in faith as
    a child, it cannot be done as an adult.   T   F

Chapter 2

TURNING TO GOD

(1)   Full acceptance of Jesus implies a very radical change in our lives. It is not at all certain that every person who is baptized, who says he is a Christian or who acts like a Christian has really made this change. In English we use the words "conversion" and "repentance" for two aspects of this deep change which is essential if one is to be a true Christian. In this chapter we will search for a full understanding and a real acceptance of what it means to accept conversion and repentance into our lives.

Unless You Change

(2)   On the occasion when Jesus was asked the important question, "Who is the greatest in the kingdom of heaven?" i.e., among those who truly accept God, we read:

So he called a little child to him and set the child in front of them. Then he said, "I tell you solemnly, unless you change and become like little children, you will never enter the kingdom of heaven! (Mt 18:2-3)

(3)   The Greek word which we translate as "change" in this passage means to turn something around in the

opposite direction, to wheel a horse or an army around. It was used to describe what one wrestler does when he succeeds in twisting the other around in the opposite direction. So, as given us by our Lord, this word means that unless a man recognizes that his direction in life is wrong, and unless he then vigorously turns it in the opposite direction, he will never enter the kingdom of heaven. Meeting Jesus involves this.

(4) Have we ever converted, changed, turned ourselves completely toward Jesus? Perhaps some of us thought that we could follow Jesus satisfactorily just by believing certain truths and by doing certain good acts. Following Jesus demands that, but it demands *much more;* it calls for a deep change, a radical turning about, a total commitment of our lives to Jesus.

And Become Like Little Children

(5) The result of the change will be that we become *as little children.* We will develop the simplicity and freedom of a secure child. The secure child is enveloped in and controlled by one experience — the experience of his parents' love and his love for them. Everything else is secondary and everything else is in place behind and because of this basic experience.

If we have once deeply turned to Jesus and continue in that direction, we too will be "like little children"—secure, hiding nothing because we have nothing to hide. We will be turned in one direction and secure in it. We will have changed in the deep and demanding way Jesus asked of all his followers: ". . . unless you change . . ."

But this is not easy; it implies a total surrender to God's will. We are not trying any longer to make God fit into our ideas; we are rather making ourselves fit into God's ideas.

(6) **A prayer:**

Lord, Jesus, without you I can do nothing,
but by your power I can do all things.
Give me now the power of your grace to turn
away completely from everything that is opposed
to the will of my loving Father. Show me how to
commit my whole life completely to you.

You Must Turn to God

(7) When Peter and John worked a miracle by the power of Jesus so that a cripple walked, we read that "everyone came running toward them in great excitement." Peter took the opportunity to tell them what they should do:

"Now you must repent and *turn to God.*" (Acts 3:19)

Later in this chapter we shall look at the word "repent," but we will try to think prayerfully here about the words "turn to God."

(8) In St. Luke's writings (he wrote the Acts), the word "conversion" is a "turning" toward the person who is announced as the Lord. It is never a call to turn toward the Church, the faith, nor even to baptism. The Lord is the only one to whom we can convert.

St. Luke presents *conversion* as something we must do

with total freedom; it is never something done to us. Conversion is a free, personal and radical offering of one's
whole self to God. Have we ever done this? Have *you* ever
done it? Or have you perhaps drifted along since your
childhood doing Christian things? Have you ever given
yourself completely to Jesus?

And Renounce Everything

(9) The meaning of this "turning to God" or conversion is
     very clear when we listen to Jesus' own words to *all*
his followers.

> *Then to all he said, "If anyone wants to be a follower*
> *of mine, let him renounce himself and take up his cross*
> *every day and follow me. For anyone who wants to*
> *save his life will lose it; but anyone who loses his life*
> *for my sake will save it."* (Lk 9:24)

Nothing could be more radical than renouncing oneself, but
this is what conversion to Jesus calls for. Nothing less will
do. To lose one's life for the sake of Jesus is demanded of
all of us. This does not necessarily imply physical death but
it does imply letting oneself go unquestioningly to Jesus and
the guidance of his Holy Spirit just as a secure child acts
toward a loving parent. Each of us must ask whether we
have ever accepted Jesus completely *on his terms* without
any conditions or reservations whatsoever? This is the very
heart of what it means to *turn to God*.

(10) Sometimes this turning to God may demand a very
     painful decision:

> *Do you suppose that I am here to bring peace on earth?*
> *No, I tell you, but rather division. For now a household*

of five will be divided; three against two and two against three . . . (Lk 12:51-52)

For or Against Jesus?

(11) Unlike other religious or civic leaders, Jesus will not accept fringe friendship. Deep down in our hearts each of us must have made a decision for him or against him. We may fail to live out this decision at times when we sin, but the decision must be made at the deepest level of our personality:

He who is not with me is against me; and he who does not gather with me scatters. (Lk 11:23)

(12) So, we cannot spend our lives merely *thinking* about Jesus, *wondering* about his claims, *debating* about his existence, *discussing* his demands. He does not call for mere interest or admiration or study of his life; he calls for *decision* about his claims and *conversion* to him as a real living and loving person. Our response must never be faint or flickering; it has to be a blazing fire within us:

I have come to bring fire on earth, and how I wish it were blazing already! (Lk 12:49)

Conversion Every Day

(13) We often use the word "conversion" about something that happened once and in the past. Jesus said it must continue to take place "every day" (Lk 9:23). Real friendship is always growing; true love is always new. A genuine relationship is changing every day as one gradually dies to one's own selfishness and lives more for the other. So it is with Christian conversion. It is growing, dynamic and

always different because it deepens every day as we discover anew the lovableness of Jesus.

(14) At the first adult conversion one's life turns to God,
        but it must be locked on him permanently. We must
frequently *take readings* to check if we are on course
toward him with increasing momentum each day. Just as
the entire life of my body will cease if my heart stops, so
too will my faith die if this inner dynamism of conversion
ever ceases.

Repentance

(15) It would be strange to set one's face in a new direction
        and then remain stationary. Usually we begin to walk
in the new direction. By true conversion we begin to walk
in the way of the Lord. We commence and continue a life-
time walk with Jesus to God our Father. This means a
walking away from sin. This is *repentance*. No Catholic
denies the necessity of acknowledging his sinfulness. But
we may have seen the sacrament of Penance as removing
this sinfulness. At times we may have forgotten that sinfulness is our permanent state before God and that consequently we must be in a permanent state of repentance
before him too.

(16) Any deep renewal of our Christian lives must begin
        with a renewal in repentance. This means a re-
discovery of the sinful state into which we were born. Only
then will we fully appreciate the continual mercy God offers
us through Jesus who died for our sins.

(17) When Jesus came, St. Mark records his first words
        for us:

Repent and believe the Good News. (Mk 1:15)

We who want to follow Jesus must understand and accept this call for repentance and accept it permanently in our lives.

We are told about his Church:

So they set off to preach repentance. (Mk 6:12)

And the Church has never forgotten to do this. Response to the call to repentance is essential to being a Christian.

Mary's Example

(18) Mary was conceived without sin but this was not through any merits on her part, nor because she had no need of redemption. No, her immaculate conception was due to the mercy of God. It was brought about by the foreseen redeeming death of Jesus. She had no need to repent of personal sin, but she did acknowledge the mercy of God by repentant love.

My spirit exults in God my savior; because he has looked upon his lowly handmaid. (Lk 1:47)

(19) Her love for us has led her to exhort us to continual prayer and penance and to say after each meditation on the mysteries of her Son:

O Jesus, forgive us our sins, save us from the fires of hell, and lead all souls to heaven especially those who have most need of your mercy.

Recalling Our Sins

(20) Often at the beginning of Mass we say, "Let us call

to mind our sins." This is not a call to dredge up our past forgiven sins in dreary detail nor is it meant to be a continual doubt about our past confessions. But we have sinned and we must be sorry for this. We know that having confessed them we are forgiven and that this forgiveness was not a grudging one. Our heavenly Father wants to forgive more than we want to be forgiven. Here is how he sees and treats us when we sin and are sorry:

While he was still a long way off, his father saw him and was moved with pity. He ran to the boy, clasped him in his arms and kissed him tenderly . . . his father said, "Quick! bring out the best robe and put it on him; put a ring on his finger and sandals on his feet. Bring the calf we have been fattening, and kill it; we are going to have a feast, a celebration, because my son was dead and has come back to life; he was lost and is found." (Lk 15:20-24)

This is God's reaction when we approach the sacrament of his mercy. Our sins, once repented of, glorify God by helping us to recognize his endless mercy.

Sinfulness More Than Sin

(21) Sin is much deeper and very much wider than the usual list which we find in books. This is not the fault of those who wrote the books but it is because sin is such a wide concept and all-embracing word. It covers each and every failure to make a full and generous response to God in any aspect of our lives. To the extent that I am not a "full" saint, to that extent I am a sinner. Here is how Jesus put it:

So with you: when you have done all you have been told

to do, say, "we are merely servants; we have done no
more than our duty." (Lk 17:9)

Or as God put on the lips of the psalmist in the Old
Testament:

Yahweh,* hear my prayer,
listen to my pleading,
answer me faithfully, righteously;
do not put your servant on trial,
no one is virtuous by your standards. (Ps 143:1-3)

(22) It is clear then that our repentance must be much
wider and far deeper than our actual sins. In the
prayer we all use, we are reminded to say that we have
sinned not only in what we have done, but "in what I have
failed to do." Our hearts must never be fully satisfied with
our service of God. We are, as it were, sinners forever, and
forever in need of repentance as we continually reach out
for the mercy of the Lord in Jesus Christ our savior.

(23) This is basically the sorrow we feel when we recognize
that we have failed to respond with the love of our
whole heart, soul, mind and strength to the God who loved
us so much "that he gave his only Son" (Jn 3:16). Our
response in love is always less than that. For this we must
be continually repentant.

---

* *Yahweh* is Hebrew for "God." Literally it means "He is." God's
name as revealed to Moses was "I am" (Ex 3:14). Israel there-
after referred to God as *Yahweh* (i.e., "He is"), a name which
expressed God's absolute and unchangeable being in all his perfection and power.

We Are Redeemed Sinners

(24)

*Sin entered the world through one man, and through
sin, death, and thus death has spread through the
whole human race because everyone has sinned . . .
by one man's disobedience, many were made
sinners . . .* (Rom 5:12, 19)

By our membership in the human race, we all, as it were,
applauded Adam's rejection of God and then confirmed it
by personal sin.

Thus deep down and *of ourselves,* we are helplessly and
hopelessly in a sinful state. That is why St. Paul was able
to write:

*I know of nothing good living in me—living, that is,
in my unspiritual self.* (Rom 7:18)

or as another translation puts it:

*No principle of good dwells in me, that is, in my natural
self.*

Of course, we rejoice that through the love of God and
our faith in Jesus we are now redeemed. But we must
never forget our need of continual redemption which comes
to us through the "grace of our Lord and savior Jesus
Christ."

Power in the Struggle Against Sin

(25) In our lives this sinfulness shows itself as it did in the
life of St. Paul, in a struggle against our best intentions:

I cannot understand my own behavior. I fail to carry

*out the things I want to do, and I find myself doing the
very things I hate . . . instead of doing the good things
I want to do, I carry out the sinful things I do not want.
When I act against my will, it is not my true self doing
it, but sin which lives in me . . . what a wretched
man I am!* (Rom 7:14, 24)

He continues:

*Who will rescue me from this body doomed to death?
Thanks be to God through Jesus Christ our Lord.*
(Rom 7:24-25)

    We give great honor to God when we accept the fact
that we are sinful and in need of Christ's redeeming power
at each moment of our lives. He said:

*My grace is enough for you:
My power is at its best in weakness.* (2 Cor 12:9)

Pharisee or Publican?

(26) Have you ever found yourself adding up the good
    things you do for God, namely, that you are honest,
generous, kind, pure and truthful? Maybe you thanked
God for this and left it at that. Maybe too, at some time,
you discovered yourself quietly condemning someone who
did not appear to have these virtues. This was a mistake
because we can never presume that we are more pleasing in
God's sight than others. God looks at behavior but he looks
beyond it; he looks into our hearts and knows them fully.

    A thought to ponder: Try to discover what it was about
the hearts of the two men in this story which made Jesus

give us the decision he did.

(27)

> *He spoke the following parable to some people who*
> *prided themselves on being virtuous and despised*
> *everyone else. "Two men went up to the Temple to*
> *pray, one a Pharisee, the other a tax collector. The*
> *Pharisee stood there and said this prayer to himself,*
> *'I thank you, God, that I am not grasping, unjust,*
> *adulterous like the rest of mankind, and particularly*
> *that I am not like this tax collector here. I fast twice*
> *a week; I pay tithes on all I get.' The tax collector*
> *stood some distance away, not daring even to raise his*
> *eyes to heaven; but he beat his breast and said, 'God*
> *be merciful to me, a sinner.' This man I tell you, went*
> *home again at rights with God; the other did not. For*
> *everyone who exalts himself will be humbled, but the*
> *man who humbles himself will be exalted."* (Lk 18:9-14)

(28) The Pharisee was not lying; he did in fact have many
good acts to his credit. Nor was the other pretending
with a false humility; apparently he believed what he said,
namely, that he was a sinner. The reason for God's decision cannot have been in their behavior; it was to be found
in their hearts. One heart was a repentant one, a humble
one; the other was not. The Pharisee although doing right
and good things forgot his own sinfulness, his own need for
God's abiding mercy. The Publican did not forget it: "God
be merciful to me a sinner."

This has to be the permanent prayer of every really
sincere Christian. It must come from a repentant heart
which recognizes that it is helpless without the saving work
of Jesus. This is especially true when we are not aware

of any specific sin and when we feel that we have done all that God has told us to do. It is then that the danger is greatest and that true repentance of the heart may leave us.

Acknowledge the Mercy of God

(29) This repentant posture of heart glorifies God because by it we recognize that Jesus is our merciful redeemer; we sing the mercies of the Lord permanently in our hearts. Every time I acknowledge my sinfulness, I acknowledge my need for being saved, my need for redemption, my need for Jesus' saving work. By doing this I glorify the loving kindness of God.

Then too the Eucharistic Prayer will mean so much more to me:

> *Even when he disobeyed you and lost your friendship you did not abandon him to the power of death; but helped all men to seek and find you. Again and again you offered a covenant to man, and through the prophets taught him to hope for salvation. Father, you so loved the world that in the fullness of time you sent your only Son to be our Savior.* (Eucharistic Prayer 4)

Are You Virtuous?

(30) Not to be called by Jesus would make life unlivable for those who know that he is the Lord, God himself.
   I did not come to call the virtuous, but sinners. (Mk 2:17)

In this quotation he lays down the first condition of our being called to him, namely, that we are self-acknowledged

sinners and that we don't consider ourselves virtuous. It
is not easy to avoid counting one's virtues occasionally and
at the same time feeling that they are something which one
has acquired by personal effort alone. Having virtues is
admirable, but attributing them to oneself in any way would
appear to put us outside those called by Jesus. We would
be among those who "prided themselves on being virtuous."
He came to call only acknowledged sinners, those who
repent. In one place we read that Jesus

> *Began to reproach the town in which most of his
> miracles had been worked, because they refused to
> repent.* (Mt 11:20)

St. John put it this way to all Christians:

> *If we say we have no sin in us, we are deceiving our-
> selves and refusing to admit the truth.* (1 Jn 1:8)

Unless you admit your sins and sinfulness, you cannot be
called by Jesus.

What Repentance Is Not

(31) (1) *Repentance is not permanent anxiety:* This is a
feeling of guilt when there is no reason for it, as
one might become obsessed with the thought that
there are germs on one's hands which therefore
need nonstop washing. This type of guilt is ac-
companied by almost permanent anxiety and of
course is not Christian because it is basically
selfish. It can be removed by prayer, sincere
admission and acceptance of one's sinfulness and
in some cases calls for professional Christian
counseling.

(32) (2) *Repentance is not dissatisfaction with one's weaknesses:* This too is fundamentally selfish and is not directed toward God nor has it real sorrow for sin in the Christian sense.

(33) (3) *Repentance is not merely being sure one is a sinner:* This can be present simply on the evidence of my life. I can know I am a sinner, but unless this leads to sincere sorrow for the sin, it is in my head and not in my heart.

(34) (4) *Repentance is not merely doing acts of penance:* Acts of penance are important but the Pharisees fasted and prayed and had many ceremonies of purification yet they never repented. Let us remember what Jesus said:

> *If your virtue goes no deeper than that of the scribes and Pharisees, you will never get into the kingdom of heaven.* (Mt 5:20)

(35) (5) *Repentance is not merely discomfort at breaking a law:* This is legal guilt and good insofar as it goes, but Christian guilt results from knowing that one has failed a friend who is God. It is far beyond law the breaking of which may lead to regret and punishment, but not necessarily to Christian repentance.

(36) (6) *Repentance is not recalling past sins:* Recognizing that we are sinners does not imply the necessity of dredging up past sins which have been repented of. The fact that we have offended God

does not mean that we have to recall the details
of past sins which might lead to further temptations.

(37)   (7) *Repentance is not going frequently to the sacrament of Penance:* This is a very good practice
under the conditions which we shall outline later.
But it could also be motivated by any of the
above kinds of guilt, rather than by a sincere
desire to meet Jesus and to express our personal
sorrow for sin and our need for his mercy.

None of these is "the repentance that leads to life" (Acts
11:18).

Fruits of True Repentance

(38) A truly repentant attitude of heart will lead to *confession* of sin:

At last I admitted to you I had sinned;
no longer concealing my guilt,
I said, "I will go to Yahweh
and confess my fault."
And you, you have forgiven the wrong I did,
have pardoned my sin. (Ps 32:5)

Regular confession is an important expression of genuine
repentance.

A truly repentant attitude is a *willingness to forsake sin.*

The Book of Proverbs tells us:

He who conceals his faults will not prosper; he who

confesses and renounces them will find mercy. (Prv 28:13)

and John the Baptist said:

If you are repentant, produce the appropriate fruit. (Mt 3:8)

(39) A truly repentant attitude of heart uses *the power of the Risen Christ against sin.*

There is nothing else, whether it be good intentions, strong willpower or frequent examination of conscience which can help us overcome sin. It can be done only by constant dependence on God's power. In his efforts, St. Paul said:

All I want is to know Christ and the power of his resurrection and to share his suffering by reproducing the pattern of his death. (Phil 3:10)

We can all reproduce the pattern of Christ's death in our own lives by calling on the power of his resurrection in our struggles against sin. In doing this we are simply sharing in the already won victory of Christ.

Repentance Is a Gift from God

(40) Repentance is not something which we can call up by human effort. It is a grace, a gift from God:

God can grant . . . the repentance that leads to life. (Acts 11:18)

He alone can grant it and he always will if we ask with faith. If our sense of sin is not strong we should often pray for this important grace.

The Sacrament of Repentance

(41) In the past some preachers and teachers tended to
     overstress the need for the detailed confession of our
sins. This sometimes caused a lack of emphasis on the most
important aspect of the sacrament, namely, genuine sorrow
for these sins.

This shifting of emphasis from the more important to
the less important elements of the sacrament tended to
reduce it to a type of spiritual dry cleaning. This may be
the reason why many people are finding that confession
does not have the fruit it is designed to have in their lives,
and why they cease approaching it with the regularity of
their childhood days.

(42) An honest review of our attitude to this sacrament
     can help each one of us. It is only when we have by
the grace of God fully accepted our sinfulness and fully
developed an attitude of Christian repentance in our hearts
that we can appreciate this sacrament of God's pardon and
peace. We must prepare for it every time by asking for
deep repentance.

(43) In the plan of God, this sacrament is meant to be, first
     of all, a meeting of friends. It is a meeting between
Christ and the Christian. Christ is present not only as a
friend but as God and as a forgiving savior. The Christian
is present as a repentant friend bringing repentant love. The
sins are secondary. Their confession is a sign of the repentance of the Christian heart just as a handshake might be
the sign of an attempt to renew friendship that has been
broken or weakened. In his turn, Christ offers the sure

sign of forgiveness in the words of the priest giving absolution.

(44) Our confession of sins must then be deep and not merely on the surface. It cannot be made from a list in a book or from a list drawn up in childhood days. "Bless me Father for I am a sinner" would be a better beginning than "Bless me Father for I have sinned" because it is closer to the full truth. Then our confession should be an unhurried review of how we are and how we are not serving God in our way of life. It might be usefully done as a talk with God, helped by the priest, as one sees Jesus by faith before him.

Confession then expresses *repentance* but it is also one of the best means of renewing our deep *conversion* to the Lord.

"God, Be Merciful to Me a Sinner"

(45) This is the ideal Christian prayer of repentance. Say it slowly now:

Have mercy on me, O God, in your goodness,
in your great tenderness wipe away my faults;
wash me clean of my guilt,
purify me from my sin.

For I am well aware of my faults,
I have my sin constantly in mind,
having sinned against none other than you,
having done what you regard as wrong.

You are just when you pass sentence on me,
blameless when you give judgment.

You know I was born guilty,
a sinner from the moment of conception.

Yet, since you love sincerity of heart,
teach me the secrets of wisdom.
Purify me with hyssop until I am clean;
wash me until I am whiter than snow.

Instill some joy and gladness into me,
let the bones you have crushed rejoice again.
Hide your face from my sins,
wipe out all my guilt.

God, create a clean heart in me,
put into me a new and constant spirit,
do not banish me from your presence,
do not deprive me of your holy spirit.

Be my savior again, renew my joy,
keep my spirit steady and willing;
and I shall teach transgressors the way to you,
and to you the sinners will return.

Save me from death, God my savior,
and my tongue will acclaim your righteousness;
Lord, open my lips,
and my mouth will speak out your praise.

Sacrifice gives you no pleasure,
were I to offer holocaust, you would not have it.
My sacrifice is this broken spirit,
you will not scorn this crushed and broken heart.

Show your favor graciously to Zion,
rebuild the walls of Jerusalem.
Then there will be proper sacrifice to please you

—holocaust and whole oblation—
and young bulls to be offered on your altar. (Ps 51)

As you pray this often ask God for the posture of heart which inspired it in King David who composed it.

POINTS FOR DISCUSSION

1. What is involved in accepting Jesus completely on *his* terms?

2. "Some Catholics have drifted along since childhood doing Christian acts, without giving themselves completely to Jesus." What do you think of this statement?

3. Compare the first words of Jesus' public life (Mk 1:15) and the first mission of the apostles (Mk 6:12) with Peter's instruction to the first Christian converts (Acts 2:38). What thought is common to all three?

4. What do you see as the fruits of true repentance?

REVIEW

1. Every baptized person is fully Christian.   T   F

2. Becoming a Christian involves a very deep change.   T   F

3. Christians must be childish in the way they act.   T   F

4. Christians must be childlike in their hearts.   T   F

5. Being born into a Catholic family makes one a Christian.   T   F

6. Conversion is only for those who are non-Catholics.   T   F

7. Conversion is what someone else does for you when they convert you.   T   F

8. Discussing Christianity makes one a better Christian.   T   F

9. Discussing Christ's claims makes one a better Christian.   T   F

10. Conversion must continue to take place every day of one's life.   T   F

11. Jesus' first public words were "Love one another."   T   F

12. The first apostles set out to preach repentance.   T   F

13. Mary's heart was not a repentant one.   T   F

14. Frequently recalling our sins is a good idea.   T   F

15. God is more anxious to forgive than we are to be forgiven.   T   F

16. Sin and sinfulness are the same thing.   T   F

17. Our love of God will always be short of his love for us.   T   F

18. God is more concerned with our hearts than our actions.   T   F

19. To consider myself better than anyone else is always wrong.   T   F

20. To be always anxious about past sins is real repentance.   T   F

21. Repentance is merely to recognize my sins.   T   F

22. True repentance leads to sincere confession of sinfulness and sins. T   F

23. I can get true repentance only by asking for it in prayer.   T   F

24. The sacrament of Penance is merely a way of getting rid of sins.   T   F

Chapter 3

A LIVING FAITH

"Strengthen in faith and love your pilgrim Church on earth . . ."

(1)   We pray these words together in the Eucharistic Prayer of the Mass. We also respond to the priest's exhortation to proclaim the mystery of faith after the consecration. We pray for the dead "whose faith is known to God alone." And of course we make a public profession of our faith when we stand to recite the Creed. Faith is fundamental to the Christian life; every Catholic is aware of its importance. This chapter is about the meaning of faith in your life. But most of all it is to help you grow in faith.

(2)   Faith means different things to different people. It is something which most of us have taken for granted — we just "have the faith" and that's that. But the suddenness of change in the secular world and the parallel changes in some aspects of the Church have forced us to think more deeply about this fundamental reality in our lives — our faith. We find that we must ask ourselves such questions as "Have I got the faith?" "Am I losing the faith?" "Have my children got the faith?" or even "How important is faith?" and, of course, "What is faith?"

Make Sure You Are in the Faith

(3)   We should not be afraid to ask these questions and to
        search for the answers. We have no choice but to look
at these questions today. We should not have any fear in
asking them, nor any doubts about the wisdom of finding
adequate answers. When writing to Christians like ourselves at Corinth, St. Paul reminded them to ask themselves similar questions. He wrote:

> *Examine yourselves to make sure you are in the faith;
> test yourselves. . . .* (2 Cor 13:5)

(4)   Obviously then, he thought it wise that people who
        were already Christians should check on their faith.
You and I may be practicing Catholics but it is still good
to do just what St. Paul encouraged the Corinthian Christians to do — to examine ourselves to make sure we are in
the faith, to test ourselves.

Is Your Faith Growing?

(5)   Presuming that we have the faith, we know that it
        can be built up and strengthened by looking at its
deeper meaning once again. As we examine it together,
we can purify it of any elements which should not be in it.
This is what St. Paul prayed for when he thought of the
Thessalonian Christians:

> *We are earnestly praying night and day to be able to
> see you face to face again and make up for any short-
> comings in your faith.* (1 Thes 3:10)

We too may have shortcomings in our faith.

(6)   In his second letter to them, he was able to write this:

> *We feel we must be continually thanking God for you,*
> *brothers; quite rightly, because your faith is growing*
> *so wonderfully. . . .* (2 Thes 1:3)

Our faith can grow wonderfully too but only if we are
clear just what faith is and what it is not. "Shortcomings"
in our faith can be made up only if we are to recognize
what they might be.

Faith in a Time of Change

(7)   Since faith is so fundamental to the Christian life, it
       is in this area that most concern appears when things
change, when, for instance, "the Mass is so different," "the
young priests have no clerical collars," "the rosary is not
said in some churches," and "Benediction is rarely seen."
But if we are sure just what faith is and have it deeply,
then changes which don't affect the fundamentals of the
Christian life will not worry us too much.

(8)   On the other hand, if our faith is a little unreal in
       parts, or if we are not sure what faith is, or what it is
not, we will worry a lot when changes come. Some are
worried by changes in the fasting laws of the Church or
because it is now lawful, in certain circumstances with due
permission, for Catholics to marry in another church.
Others may be worried when Christians who are not Catholics are allowed, again with due permission and guarantee,
to receive Holy Communion during Mass. Knowing what
faith is and having it healthily help us to accept changes
without fear. But first let us remind ourselves again how
important faith is and how nothing can take its place.

Importance of Faith

(9)   In the epistle to the Hebrews we are told:

Now it is impossible to please God without faith. . . .
(Heb 11:6)

When some of his followers hesitated about staying with him Jesus himself said:

I tell you most solemnly, everyone who believes has eternal life. (Jn 6:47)

And in his letter to the Galatians, St. Paul writes:

We acknowledge that what makes a man righteous is not obedience to the law, but faith in Jesus Christ.
(Gal 2:15)

After Paul's and Silas' miraculous escape from prison, the jailer asked them, "Sirs, what must I do to be saved?" (Acts 16:30) To which they replied:

Become a believer in the Lord Jesus, and you will be saved, and your household too. (Acts 16:31)

And among the last words of Jesus to his Church are these:

Go out to the whole world; proclaim the Good News to all creation. He who believes and is baptized will be saved; he who does not believe will be condemned.
(Mk 16:16)

(10) To believe in God is to have faith in him. Without this faith nothing is helpful; nothing will take its place. Not even going to Mass regularly, not even frequent prayer or even being baptized. Faith is much more important than any of these; and indeed without it, none of these have any value to us. Faith is the foundation; it is the

groundwork; it is the rock on which we must build.

Listening and Understanding

(11) When Jesus spoke to the men of his time, they all listened to him, but not all understood him. He said of some of them:

> *They look without seeing and listen without hearing or understanding.* (Mt 13:13)

In the question of faith, it is easy enough to listen, but to understand is a gift from God. Pray that you may understand his word in this chapter in the way he wants you to.

Faith Is Friendship

(12) It will help us in the understanding and appreciation of faith, if we look at friendship, because faith is basically a friendship. It is like any friendship, a felt relationship between two people, in this case between God and man. And it is best to use the example of friendship between a parent and child. This is the example which Jesus gave us. It is difficult to analyze any friendship because of its beautiful simplicity, but perhaps this is the illness of modern life that it seems necessary to look again at both friendship and faith in this way. God's own words are:

(13)
> *As a hen gathers her chicks under her wings.*
> (Mt 23:37)

> *Can a woman forget her baby at the breast?* (Is 49:15)

> *Your heavenly Father knows.* (Mt 6:32)

This is how God loves you and me. He loves us as a parent loves a child. It is here that faith begins.

Parent and Child

(14) In the friendship between parent and child, four
things take place. The parent offers signs of love such
as words, gifts, embracing, feeding, working for, kissing,
caring for, etc. The child hears, sees and feels these signs
and acknowledges them by his or her own signs such as
words, embraces or simple smiles in return. The child then
responds further by a total trust in everything the father
or mother says and finally acts on that trust by obeying the
loving father and mother and stepping out in faith on their
words in real life.

Let us look at these steps in friendship taken by the
child because they are the identical steps in faith taken by
the Christian adult. Here they are again:

The parent reveals his or her love in *signs*.
The child *accepts* what the signs are saying — "You love
me."
The child *trusts* what the signs are saying — "I trust
you."
The child *acts* on what the signs say — "I obey you."

(15) *The Parent's Signs:* A loving father or mother has no
other way to show love than in signs, like words and
gestures. These are so important because no child — or
indeed anyone — could guess at love unless it is somehow
shown in signs. A simple "I love you" or a mother's smile,
or the love demonstrated in feeding or toilet training are
the signs offered the child of something deeper, namely,
the loving heart of his or her father or mother.

(16) *The Child Accepts:* If you have ever watched the

child, even a very young baby, respond to his mother,
you will appreciate every child's ability to hear, to accept
and to acknowledge the signs offered by a loving parent.
The child's response differs as he grows older, but in hun-
dreds of little ways he does acknowledge the love of his parents, not the least of which is simply to say, "I know you
love me."

(17) *The Child Trusts:* We have all seen damaged persons who cannot trust anyone. Usually this has happened through a defective relationship with parents. As
children, these persons did not learn to trust their parents
very early in life. But most children do trust their parents
very fully. They believe you; they take your words for "gospel," they cannot imagine — until it happens a few times —
that mother or father can tell them a lie. A child's natural
inclination is to trust parents.

(18) *The Child Acts* on the parents' words. The child's
trust is not just in his heart and much less in his head.
In a very real sense it is in his feet. He is prepared to step
out once a loving father or mother assures him it is safe.
His trust is shown by actions which sometimes surprise us.
Children will disbelieve the whole world if it contradicts
what a parent says; they will do dangerous things if they
can hold a parent's hand while doing it. Because they lack
emotional and impulse control, they will not always do as
they are told, but their little hearts feel more comfortable
in obeying than in disobeying.

The Heart of a Child

(19) At this moment, we may seem to have come a long
way from the meaning of faith, but on the contrary,

we are very close to just what it means to live a life of faith.

So he called a little child to him and set the child in front of them. Then he said, "I tell you solemnly, unless you change and become like little children you will never enter the kingdom of heaven. And so, the one who makes himself as little as this little child is the greatest in the kingdom of heaven." (Mt 18:2-4)

This is like an ultimatum; it *is* an ultimatum. Jesus says, "Unless you become like little children, you will never enter the kingdom of heaven." Unless and until we have the heart of a child before our heavenly Father, we cannot enter heaven because we have not faith.

(20) Why does a child read the signs of his father's or mother's love so easily? Why does he respond in acknowledgment so readily? Why can he trust the word of a parent so simply? And why is a child willing to step out on a father's or mother's promise without a moment of doubt? These four questions have the same answer. It is because a child's heart is simple and trusts, is naturally hopeful, ready to express his needs to someone who can satisfy them and wants to obey someone who deserves obedience. This is the heart of a child. When I have this posture of heart, I am ready for friendship and ready for faith. With this attitude of simplicity, trust, hope and readiness to express my needs to God, to trust and obey him, I am ready for the gift of faith.

Let us apply these four steps of a child before a parent to our own relationship with God.

Do You See God's Signs?

(21) Because he is a person, or rather three persons, God
  can communicate his love with other persons only
through *signs*. Down the centuries we read that in the Old
Testament:

> *At various times in the past and in various different*
> *ways, God spoke to our ancestors through the prophets.*
> (Heb 1:1)

The signs he used were creation of the world, thunder,
lightning, the sun, the stars, men's dreams, manna in the
desert, and then the prophets. These were the signs of
God's fatherly love and concern for his people. He continued to show them that he was their God and they were
his people.

As we say during Mass:

(22)
> *Again and again you offered a covenant to man.*
> (Eucharistic Prayer 4)

Finally, God offered the great sign of his love. He spoke
his final word when

> *The word was made flesh,*
> *He lived among us, (pitched his tent among us)*
> *and we saw his glory,*
> *the glory that is his as the only Son of the Father,*
> *full of grace and truth.* (Jn 1:14)

This Word is Jesus, God's supreme sign of his fatherly love
for man. Jesus is God's Word, God's smile, God's embrace,
God's handshake, God's gift, God's grace (something un-
earned), to us. And so we know that:

of all the names in the world given to men,
this is the only one by which we can be saved. (Acts
4:12)

(23) Or as Jesus himself said:

I tell you most solemnly, whoever listens to my words,
and believes in the one who sent me, has eternal life.
(Jn 5:24)

And as the Father said:

This is my Son, the Beloved; my favor rests on him.
(Mt 3:17)

Ask yourself: Do I acknowledge Jesus as God's Son and
the sign of God's love for me? Do I acknowledge it deeply?
This is the beginning of faith.

Do You Accept God's Signs?

(24) Despite the signs given them on the journey to the
promised land, many of his people refused to have
faith in God's fatherly protection:

They put Yahweh to the test saying, "Is Yahweh with
us, or not?" (Ex 17:7)

We can do the same. We can see the signs of God's love
but neglect them.

(25) When Jesus came, he offered his miracles to show
that he was God's messenger and to strengthen the
faith of those who witnessed them. To those who demanded
further signs he pointed to his coming resurrection as the
last sign upon the acceptance or rejection of which men
will be saved or lost. Here is how St. Paul puts it to us:

> *If your lips confess that Jesus is Lord and if you*
> *believe in your heart that God raised him from the dead,*
> *then you will be saved.* (Rom 10:9)

Do we believe this in our hearts and confess it on our lips?

Although he came as God's sign of fatherly protection for men, some acknowledged him and some did not. Some men said:

> *You are the Christ, the Son of the living God.* (Mt. 16:17)

(26) Others said:

> *He is possessed by a devil. . . .* (Jn 8:48)

Others simply ignored him. Finally some men put nails through Jesus' outreaching hands — refused to acknowledge God's greatest sign. What is *your* response?

(27) In your name your parents and godparents acknowledged Jesus as God's sign of salvation at your baptism. As an adult you must make that acknowledgment for yourself expressing the inner commitment of your heart. It is good to pause for a moment and do it now in prayer.

(28) As Christians we must take a clear and definite stand in answer to Jesus' question:

> *But you, who do you say I am?* (Mt 16:16)

Jesus says to each of us:

> *If you know (i.e., acknowledge) me, you know my Father*
> *too. From this moment you know him and have seen*
> *him. . . . You must believe me when I say that I am in*
> *the Father and the Father is in me.* (Jn 14:7,11)

and then he assures us:

*. . . the Father himself loves you for loving me and
believing that I came from God.* (Jn 16:27)

How deeply do I believe that Jesus came out from God
for me?

(Here pause and pray about this question.)

(29) As Catholics we are aware of other signs offered by
       God, especially the Church and the sacraments, but
unless we have acknowledged God's greatest sign very
deeply and continue to do so in prayer, the other signs will
lose their value. Even the sacraments will become spiritual
slot machines instead of powerful sources of growth in
God's friendship.

(30) We have a frequent reminder to express our faith after
       the consecration at Mass as we proclaim:

Christ has died,
Christ is risen,
Christ will come again.

Or sometimes we proclaim:

Lord, by your cross and resurrection
You have set us free.
You are the savior of the world.

If we mean these prayers deeply — and only to the extent
that we mean them — we accept God's signs. But we must
go from accepting the signs of God's love to really trusting
him. Our acceptance is shown by our trust. If I say that I
believe and that I accept your love for me, you can rea-
sonably expect me to trust you.

Do You Trust God's Signs?

(31) Jesus is the Word of God; he is the Eternal Word
which God has spoken to himself for all eternity; he
is God's eternal canticle to his own greatness. He is the
one "who is nearest to the Father's heart" (Jn 1:18). He is
the word which God is continually speaking to us. He is
God's messenger to man.

To have seen me is to have seen the Father. (Jn 14-9)

*What the Father has taught me is what I preach; he
who sent me is with me, and has not left me to myself,
for I always do what pleases him.* (Jn 8:28-29)

(32) Do you trust everything Jesus said? Do you even
know everything he said? Do you know God's word?
Do you know where you find God's word? It is still being
spoken in the world by Jesus living in the Church and in
each of us by his Spirit. And the Church offers us God's
written word in the scriptures. Do we read the scriptures
regularly? Are we really interested in what they say?

Measuring Our Faith

Do you trust what you know of this word? Let us take
some of Jesus' words:

Anyone who listens to you, listens to me. (Lk 10:16)

Do you accept the teaching of the Church fully?

*Know that I am with you always;
yes, to end of time.* (Mt 28:20)

Are you perhaps worried that God is no longer with his
Church?

Do not let your hearts be troubled.

Trust in God still, and trust in me. (Jn 14:1)

Are you troubled as if God did not have the whole world in his hands?

(33)
That is why I am telling you not to worry about your life and what you are to eat, nor about your body and how you are to clothe it. (Mt 6:25)

Are you frequently concerned about material things despite this promise from God through Jesus? Concerned even to the point of being too busy to make time for prayer?

Peace I bequeath to you. My own peace I give you, a peace the world cannot give, this is my gift to you. (Jn 14:27)

Have you with simple faith in Jesus' word accepted this gift of peace as already yours, or are you still frantically seeking it elsewhere?

(34)
I will not leave you orphans;
I will come back to you.
In a short time the world will no longer see me;
but you will see me,
because I live and you will live.
On that day
you will understand that I am in my Father
and you in me and I in you. (Jn 14:18-20)

Do you really trust the word of Jesus that he is close to you as he is close to his Father, or do you sometimes feel you are struggling alone and unaided in living your Christian life?

Suffering is part of your training; God is treating you as his sons. Has there ever been any son whose Father did not train him? . . . We have all had our human fathers who punished us, and we respected them for it; we ought to be even more willing to submit ourselves to our spiritual Father. (Heb 12:7,9)

(35) This total trust in the words of Jesus is the test of faith. It will have the effect of liberating us, of setting us free from reliance on our own strength and policies, because we are submitting to the power and guiding word of Jesus:

To the Jews who believed in him Jesus said: "If you make my word your home you will indeed be my disciples, you will learn the truth and the truth will make you free." (Jn 8:31-32)

We make his word our "home" when we really trust and obey him.

Do You Act on God's Promises?

(36) Do I show my trust in God's word by my actions? Am I willing to take him at his word, to obey him despite the consequences for myself? When Jesus promised his body and blood under the appearance of bread and wine, many said: "This is intolerable language," and they refused to believe. Every time you receive the Eucharist, if it is an act of faith, you are stepping out on his word. At the beginning of Mass we pray:

. . . we have this bread to offer.
It will become for us the bread of life.

Then we approach the altar without hesitation about God's promise. This is trust in action.

(37) But is this so in every aspect of your life? Do you
        confess with your lips, believe in your heart and step
out with your feet? As St. Peter stood on the edge of the
boat and heard Jesus say, "Come!" he could have confessed
that Jesus was the Lord, and still stayed in the boat. It
was only when he took the first step out of the boat onto
the water that his faith became real and beyond doubt.
This was his act of trust in Jesus' word — trust in action.

(38) The centurion assured Jesus of his belief that he could
        cure his son even at a distance. He was prepared to
go home once Jesus had said the word. This was faith that
stepped out, faith in his feet, and so Jesus said to him:

> *Go back, then; you have believed, so let it be done for
> you.* (Mt 8:13)

But if he had insisted that Jesus come down until he could
see if the words about his servant's cure were true, this
would not have been faith.

(39) When the woman with the hemorrhage touched his
        cloak and was sure she would be cured simply by
doing so, this was stepping out in faith. Jesus said to her:

> *Courage, my daughter, your faith has restored you to
> health.* (Mt 9:22)

She did not merely acknowledge Jesus, nor merely trust
him; she acted on her acknowledgment and trust. This is
real faith, the only faith, faith in action. It is living faith.

(40) At Mass we speak about "Abraham our father in
        faith." He became our father in faith when he obeyed
God's command to go into the desert "not knowing where

he was going." He trusted God again when he was willing
to offer Isaac in sacrifice "confident that God had the power
even to raise the dead" (Heb 11:19). Would you do this?
That is total faith.

Faith Is Visible

(41) Works are the final test of faith. Jesus puts it to us
with great simplicity:

You are my friends, if you do what I command you.
(Jn 15:14)

The measure of our faith is the measure of our willingness
to do God's will every moment of our lives.

(42) Lest the first Christians would be in any doubt about
this St. Paul said that he had received his "apostolic
mission to preach the *obedience of faith*" (Rom 1:5).
But of course he reminds them that they get strength with
their faith for this obedience. It is not their own effort.

*Glory to him who is able to give you the strength to
live according to the Good News I preach. . . .* (Rom
16:25)

If you feel you are struggling alone, your faith is lacking.
Faith gives strength for the struggle of the Christian life.

(43) St. James puts the necessity of a living faith very
vividly when he states that faith must be a posture of
heart which steps out into good works:

(44)
*Take the case, my brothers, of someone who has never
done a single good act but claims that he has faith.*

Will that faith save him? . . . Do realize, you senseless man, that faith without good deeds is useless. . . . You see now that it is by doing something good, and not only by believing that a man is justified. (Jas 2:14, 20,24)

Faith Gives Power

(45) At the end of his life, Jesus offered this assurance against which we all could test our faith:

I tell you most solemnly, whoever believes in me will perform the same works as I do myself, he will perform even greater works, because I am going to the Father. Whatever you ask for in my name I will do, so that the Father may be glorified in the Son. If you ask for anything in my name, I will do it. (Jn 14:12-14)

(46) Do we really believe to the extent of expecting to do even *greater works* than Jesus did? We ought to be willing to step out on all of God's promises and to expect even miracles. Our attitude in this regard is one of the surest tests of our faith.

St. Paul challenged the Corinthians with that very test. He said:

Examine yourselves to make sure you are in the faith; test yourselves. Do you acknowledge that Jesus Christ is really in you? If not, you have failed the test. (2 Cor, 13:5-6)

St. Paul is saying that if we do not *act* like people who are conscious of God's power within us our faith has failed the test. Surely this is food for long and deep meditation for us all.

Degrees of Faith

(47) Jesus told the story of the sower when he wanted to tell us that while faith is offered to everyone, many respond generously, some not so generously, others only temporarily or not at all. He talked about the sower whose seed (the word of God) did not bear the same fruit (faith) because some who heard it had no roots, others let it be choked by riches and selfishness and still others let the devil take it from them. And even those who receive the word of God in genuine faith will respond well or fairly well or not so well depending on their posture of heart (Mk 4:1-9, 13-20). Each of us must ask himself if he has forgotten that faith must grow because it is a seed and not something static. It cannot be preserved like the talent which the man wrapped up and did not use (cf. Mt 25:25).

Pray that you will hear Jesus' own formula for deep faith:

As for the part (of the seed) in rich soil, this is people with a noble and generous heart who have heard the word and take it to themselves and yield a harvest through their perseverance. (Lk 8:15)

We all have need to pray for that "noble and generous heart." It is the greatest gift of all.

Faith Is God's Gift

(48) We can do nothing to earn faith. It must be sought in prayer and accepted as an undeserved gift. It usually comes through hearing the word of God, and through the experience of Christian community:

Faith comes by what is preached. (Rom 10:17)

It is by grace that you have been saved, through faith; not by anything of your own, but by a gift from God; not by anything that you have done, so that nobody can claim credit. We are God's work of art, created in Christ Jesus to live the good life as from the beginning he had meant us to live it. (Eph 2:8-10)

It is only to the childlike of heart that the gift of faith is given.

(49) The childlike heart is itself a gift. Remember Jesus' prayer?

I bless you, Father, Lord of heaven and of earth, for hiding these things from the learned and the clever and revealing them to mere children. Yes, Father, for that is what it pleased you to do. (Mt 11:25-26)

Pray every day for the heart of a child before God.

Faith Is Poverty of Spirit

(50) Christ's most important sermon was the Sermon on the Mount. It was his policy speech. Often read it all as a continuous reading. It is in Matthew's Gospel, chapters five to seven. Jesus began it this way:

How happy are the poor in spirit for theirs is the kingdom of heaven. (Mt 5:3)

This poverty of spirit means those whose heart has the right posture before God — the posture of faith. Those who are "poor in spirit" are those who know that of themselves they have nothing, cannot guide their own lives to salvation, and recognize their need for continual help of God's power. They know they are sinful and helpless to help themselves and thus they trust in God's power and guidance. They are hearts ready for the gift of faith.

— The Old Testament

(51) The holy men of the Old Testament all had this posture of heart expressed in an attitude of searching for, listening to and readiness to carry out the will of the Lord. They were totally available to their Lord because they accepted his love and the privilege he gave them of belonging to him.

> *Is there any need to say more? There is not time for me to give an account of Gideon, Barak, Samson, Jephthah or of David, Samuel and the prophets. These were men who through faith conquered kingdoms, did what is right and earned the promises. They could keep a lion's mouth shut, put out blazing fires and emerge unscathed from battle. They were weak people who were given strength. . . . These are all heroes of faith, but they did not receive what was promised, since God had made provision for us to have something better, and they were not to reach perfection except with us.* (Heb 11:32-34, 39-40)

We who have that "something better" in Christ can look also to all the saints of the Church, from Our Lady down to those of our own time, as many more witnesses to faith.

(52) Mary's faith was total. It is demonstrated in her response to God's request that she become the mother of his Son. Her final words were ones of submission, reverence and availability to do the will of God:

I am the handmaid of the Lord, let what you have said
be done to me." (Lk 1:38)

In these words, because they express perfect faith, we have
the model for the whole Church in its response to its Lord.

(53) Jesus himself gives us the example of the perfect faith-
response when, in the face of torture and death, he
prayed:

Father, if you are willing, take this cup away from me.
Nevertheless, let your will be done, not mine. (Lk
22: 42-43)

(54) When this is our posture of heart before God we will
be able to say with St. Paul:

I have been crucified with Christ, and I live now not
with my own life but with the life of Christ who lives in
me. The life I now live in this body I live in faith; faith
in the Son of God who loved me and who sacrificed
himself for my sake." (Gal 2:20)

(55) We can then exhort one another with a further passage from Hebrews:

With so many witnesses in a great cloud on every side
of us, we too, then, should throw off everything that
hinders us especially the sin that clings so easily, and
keep running steadily in the race we have started.
Let us not lose sight of Jesus, who leads us in our faith
and brings it to perfection. (Heb 12:1-2)

Through this faith, we receive God's supreme gift, the Holy
Spirit.

In the next chapter we shall think and pray about this.

A prayer:

> *Heavenly Father, give me a living faith;*
> *a faith by which I will not only accept what you teach*
> *me*
> *but also act on it every day.*
> *Give me faith to surrender myself to you*
> *in complete trust as a child to a loving parent.*
> *I commit myself completely to you now.*
> *Do with me whatever you will.*

POINTS FOR DISCUSSION

1. Discuss the following: "The faith Jesus asks for is an act of trust and self-abandonment by which we commit ourselves completely to his power and guiding word."

2. How can Christian faith be compared to a child-parent relationship?

3. What are some of the signs God has given us of his love?

4. List some of God's promises on which we should act by faith.

REVIEW

1.	One's faith can be taken for granted.	T	F
2.	It is important to make sure one is in the faith.	T	F
3.	Faith can have shortcomings and therefore grow throughout life.	T	F
4.	Deep faith gives us less fear of changes that are not fundamental.	T	F
5.	Changes in Church law endanger the faith of Christians.	T	F
6.	Without faith it is impossible to please God.	T	F
7.	A very good moral life can take the place of faith.	T	F
8.	It is possible to hear the word of God without spiritual understanding.	T	F
9.	Faith is friendship for God.	T	F
10.	A child naturally distrusts others.	T	F
11.	A child's heart easily reads the signs of a parent's love.	T	F
12.	Unless we become like little children in our hearts we cannot be saved.	T	F
13.	Any intelligent person will automatically read and accept God's signs.	T	F

14. One can listen without believing.   T   F

15. Jesus' miracles were an invitation to faith.   T   F

16. The Church and the sacraments are
    signs of God's love for us.   T   F

17. Faith must imply trust in God's words
    if it is genuine.   T   F

18. Faith can be measured by how much
    we act on God's word.   T   F

19. Our attitude to suffering can be a real
    test of how much we believe.   T   F

20. Faith receives its best test when it calls
    for stepping out on God's word.   T   F

21. Faith gives power to live the word of
    God.   T   F

22. We can get faith simply by studying a
    course in theology.   T   F

23. Reading this book will automatically
    increase one's faith.   T   F

24. Faith is a gift from God which must
    be asked for in prayer.   T   F

25. Mary's faith was expressed in her offering
    of herself completely to God.   T   F

Chapter 4

THE HOLY SPIRIT

(1)   In the last two chapters we saw that Jesus asks for
       deep repentance and a deep response in faith to his
love. These are very radical and very complete demands
on the individual. They call for a full-time and total giving
of oneself to the Lord and to others. This is like dying to
oneself. It is difficult. Have you wondered at times if this
is really all there is to the Christian life? Is it just a matter
of a continual and rather lonely effort to do what Jesus
asked us to do and to avoid what he said was sinful? If
this is how you see the Christian life, it will make you very
discouraged, very tired and maybe inclined to give up.

(2)   But there is more to the Christian life than that, much
       more. The Christian life is much more an experience
of *receiving* than a matter of giving.

Why Jesus Came
(3)   When the message of Jesus was spreading out from
       Palestine, the city of Ephesus was among the finest in
the Roman Empire. We can share the joy of St. Paul's
heart when he discovered that a small number of people in
that city had accepted the Christian message. His first

question to them was this:

Did you receive the Holy Spirit when you became believers?

They replied:

No, we were never even told there was such a thing as the Holy Spirit. (Acts 19:2-3)

(4)   They had repented and were converted, but because they lacked instruction, they had not expressed faith in the full Christian message. It is the Holy Spirit who is the fullness and perfection of this message of Jesus.

(5)   It was to give this fullness that Jesus came, as John the Baptist told his followers:

The man on whom you see the Spirit come down and rest is the one who is going to baptize you with the Holy Spirit. (Jn 1:34)

(6)   This phrase sums up the whole purpose of Jesus' coming, namely, that every one of us would be born again in the Spirit and receive the life-giving power of God in our mortal bodies.

(7)   It is this that makes the Christian life more than an attempt to do some things and to avoid others: it is this — the presence of the power of God through the Holy Spirit — that makes Christianity what it is.

(8)   The purpose of this chapter is to help you accept the Holy Spirit in your own life more fully, to experience his presence by increased power in all you do, and to enjoy the peace which he alone can give. It is meant to be a

prayerful look at what Jesus intended each of us to have when he gave us his Holy Spirit at the moment of our baptism. This is best achieved if we can look at his own words to his apostles and at the effect these words had, but more especially at the effect the Holy Spirit had on the lives of the early Christians. But let us first hear what Jesus said about the Holy Spirit.

Jesus Left His Apostles for Their Own Good

(9) Jesus' farewell address to his apostles (cf. Jn 14-17) ought to be especially dear to every Christian. It is very valuable to read it right through frequently. We will refer to it often in this chapter. It was spoken immediately after the Last Supper.

(10) Jesus had already been with his apostles for about two and a half years. During that time he had instructed them on how to live; he had given them the example of his own powerful personality. They had naturally come to depend on him, to ask him when they were in doubt, and to feel more sure of themselves when he was near them. They could hear him, touch him, see him and observe the power which went out from him to calm a roaring sea or to cast out devils. They gained courage and assurance from his physical presence. Now he was about to leave them. He told them that they would suffer many things and perhaps even be killed in the name of God.

(11) He went further and said to them:

I did not tell you this from the outset, because I was with you; but now I am going to the one who sent me. Not one of you has asked, "Where are you going?"

Yes, you are sad at heart because I have told you this.
Still, I must tell you the truth; it is for your own good
that I am going. . . . (Jn 16:4-7)

(12) We can sympathize with their feeling of sadness or
fear. They are ordinary people like ourselves who
had no wish to be expelled from the company of their fellowmen, nor to be killed by anyone in God's name. But
Jesus added that it was *for their own good* that he was
going away. If you and I understand and believe how and
why this is so, it can change our lives. He made it quite
clear that in his physical body he left us only to give us
something better. This better gift is the Holy Spirit.

(13) It was only after his death and resurrection that he
could confer this great gift on people. St. John reminds us:

. . . for there was no Spirit as yet, because Jesus had
not yet been glorified. (Jn 7:39)

(14) It is only when he is "lifted up" and has gone to the
Father that his body, glorified by this, is endowed with
divine life-giving power.

Jesus Christ, our Lord, who . . . was proclaimed Son of
God in all his power through his resurrection from the
dead. (Rom 1:4)

(15) Once he has been glorified by his heavenly Father,
power flows from him to those who believe, as from
an endless source. It is the risen Jesus who fulfills the promise to give us the great gift which can change our lives,
the gift of the Holy Spirit.

Jesus Promised to Return to His Church

(16) During his farewell address after the Last Supper, Jesus told his apostles:

I will not leave you orphans; I will come back to you.
(Jn 14:18)

Then he went on to say:

In a short time the world will no longer see me; but you will see me, because I live and you will live. On that day, you will understand that I am in my Father and you in me and I in you. *(Jn 14:18-19)*

(17) His new coming then is going to achieve a nearness which his physical presence could not accomplish; he is going to be near us as he is near his Father, i.e., in intimate personal friendship. His heavenly Father too will come to us in that same intimate way:

If anyone loves me he will keep my word,
and my Father will love him,
and we shall come to him
and make our home with him." *(Jn 14:23)*

(18) When we use the word "home" it expresses close friendship and full acceptance. This — the friendship of God the Father and of his Son Jesus — is what we are offered after the resurrection. This greatest of all gifts is the Holy Spirit, the presence and the power of God given to us.

How He Returned — His Holy Spirit

(19)
Unless I go, the Advocate will not come to you.
(Jn 16:7)

The word "advocate" means someone who is willing to help and able to do so. It means a friend who is firmly on your side. It means someone who can advise, support, protect and intercede for you. It means someone who loves you permanently and who has power to show that love in the best possible way. This is the Holy Spirit who Jesus promises will come to the members of his Church when they believe. He has this mission of love which he will express in numerous ways. We shall look at these later in this chapter.

(20) Jesus tells us that the Holy Spirit is that other advocate:

> *whom the world can never receive since it neither sees nor knows him; but you know him, because he is with you, he is in you.* (Jn 14:17)

(21) To "know" someone in scripture means to have a friendship with them; it is not merely to "know about" them. It really means love. The Holy Spirit then is God's ✓ love for us. St. Paul puts it:

> *The love of God is poured into our hearts by the Holy Spirit who has been given us.* (Rom 5:5)

(22) He is God's friendship offered to us, but unlike any other friendship it is friendship with constant power to help and it is friendship that never changes. And about this "friendship-person" Jesus assures us:

> *He is with you, he is in you.* (Jn 14:17)

He Returns With Real Power

(23) During his last instructions to his disciples before his

ascension into heaven, he renewed his great promise:

And now I am sending down to you what the Father has promised. Stay in the city then, until you are clothed with the power from on high. (Lk 24:49)

(24) Here is a promise of new power in their lives. Power is not something about which one can be mistaken easily. We either have it or not. For instance, if I can lift a chair, give a speech, run a mile, practice patience or paint a picture then I obviously have the power to do these things. If I try and fail to do these things, then equally obviously I lack the power. No amount of talking or imagining will give me power that I have not got.

(25) Let us look further at this word "power" as it appears in the New Testament. The Greek word used is the one from which we get the English words "dynamite" and "dynamo." Both these words express power which is experienced and which does not have to be imagined. In St. Luke's writings, he speaks mostly about the Holy Spirit as this kind of power, a power which can move things, get things done. So in Jesus' own words:

You will receive power when the Holy Spirit comes on you. (Acts 1:8)

(26) But did they? Take Peter, for instance. Chosen as the leader of the apostolic group, he had seen many miracles worked by Jesus and had himself walked on the water by the power of Jesus. And when Jesus spoke about his own passion and death, Peter said—"Though all lose faith in you, I will never lose faith" (Mt 26:33) and no doubt he felt sure of himself. But when a girl asked him if he was

a follower of Jesus, he denied it three times. When Jesus was arrested, Peter followed only "at a distance" (Mt 26:58) and ended up behind closed doors "for fear of the Jews." Like Peter, all the apostles were ordinary men with the fears of ordinary men; that is until they received new power into their lives.

(27) This power, the Holy Spirit, came down as Jesus promised on Pentecost Sunday, and from that room 12 men emerged. They were no longer scared, no longer weak, no longer unwilling to witness to their belief in Jesus. About the man who was scared by a servant girl we now read:

> *Then Peter stood up with the Eleven and addressed them in a loud voice: ". . . listen carefully to what I say. . . . Jesus the Nazarene. . . . You killed him, but God raised him to life."* (Acts 2:14, 22-23)

(28) Each of them then witnessed to Jesus by preaching his name everywhere and finally by dying for that name. This was not by their own power—which they clearly lacked—but by the power of God, namely, the Holy Spirit.

(29) The followers of Jesus, then, who take his word for what it says and who step out and who act on his promises, experience real power in their Christian lives as God gives them courage, consolation, words of wisdom, healings, praying in tongues or prophecy. The Spirit guided and still guides the Church in her major decisions and is our guarantee that the message of Jesus will always remain with us.

The Power Is in You

(30) When the Spirit of God was poured down on the first
     Christians, the apostles said it was but the fulfillment
of this Old Testament prophecy.

> *In the days to come — it is the Lord who speaks —*
> *I will pour out my Spirit on all mankind.* (Acts 2:17,
> cf. Jl 2:28)

(31) The prophet Ezekiel also foretold that the Spirit of
     God would be given to the new people of God. This
was recalled by St. Paul writing to the Thessalonians (I
Thes 4:8).

> *And you will know that I am Yahweh, when I open*
> *your graves and raise you from your graves, my people.*
> *And I shall put my Spirit in you, and you will live.*
> (Ez 37:14)

(32) Thus Pentecost, or the outpouring of the Spirit, is the
     inauguration of the "last time" of salvation, the time of
the Church. And because of this outpouring, the Church
has already begun its final full possession of the Spirit in
heaven.

(33) The Church is the temple of the Spirit. It is still a pil-
     grim Church carried along by the promise and fore-
taste of what will be. You are a member of that Church,
the people of God and you are a temple of the Holy Spirit:

> *Didn't you realize that you were God's temple and that*
> *the Spirit of God was living among you?* (I Cor 3:16)

Elizabeth, Zechariah, Mary, Jesus

(34) When Mary asked how the second person of the
     Blessed Trinity would become enfleshed in her womb,
this was the reply given her by God's angel:

*The Holy Spirit will come upon you and the power of
the Most High will cover you with its shadow."* (Lk
1:35)

It would be achieved by God's power, God's Holy
Spirit.

When Elizabeth met Mary with Jesus in her womb, she
was:

filled with the Holy Spirit. . . . (Lk 1:42)

(35) When Zechariah received back his power of speech at
     the circumcision of his son John, he was:

filled with the Holy Spirit and spoke this prophecy. . . .
(Lk 1:67)

When Jesus was preparing for his preaching, he was:

"filled with the Holy Spirit" and *"led by the Spirit"* to
pray and fast for forty days in "the wilderness." (Lk 4:1)

When preaching and praying to his Father, Jesus was:

filled with joy by the Holy Spirit. (Lk 10:21)

This is the Spirit he sent to us who believe; he is now
in us most intimately.

Power to Become Children of God (Jn 1:12)

(37) The presence of the Spirit in the life of believers and in the Church is always characterized then by newness, growth, development, movement, sharing and renewal (making new).

(38) Jesus by his resurrection and ascension began a new life. As God, he has perfect power to share that new life with his followers. He shares it with us by bestowing his Spirit on all who are united to him through faith and baptism. By this he makes us like himself, true sons of God. This is the new life which Jesus brings.

> *The proof that you are sons of God is that God has sent the Spirit of his Son into our hearts: the Spirit that cries out "Abba, Father," and it is this that makes you a son, you are not a slave any more; and if God has made you son, then he has made you heir . . . now that God has acknowledged you.* (Gal 4:6-9)

(39) We now belong to Christ as St. Paul told the Romans:

> *Unless you possessed the Spirit of Christ you would not belong to him.* (Rom 8:9)

(40) Belonging completely to Christ we no longer belong to ourselves. We acknowledge this in our prayers at Mass when we say in the fourth Eucharistic Prayer:

> *And that we might live no longer for ourselves*
> *   but for him,*
> *he sent the Holy Spirit from you, Father,*
> *as his first gift to those who believe.*

The supreme gift of the Holy Spirit is summed up by John:

> *But to all who did accept him, he gave power to become children of God.* (Jn 1:12)

Power to Love God and Love Like God

(41)
> *The love of God has been poured into our hearts by the Holy Spirit which has been given us.* (Rom 5:5)

The power of the Holy Spirit in us gives us the privilege of experiencing the love of God and of expressing our love in return. We merely associate ourselves with Jesus praising his Father through the Holy Spirit in us.

> *Through him,*
> *with him,*
> *in him,*
> *in the unity of the*
> *Holy Spirit,*
> *all glory and honor is yours,*
> *almighty Father,*
> *for ever and ever.* (All Eucharistic Prayers)

(42) We have the power to love God with his own love. It is a new power to pray with the prayer of Jesus to his Father about which we shall see in another lesson. By the presence of the Holy Spirit in us, we become *a living sacrifice of praise* (Eucharistic Prayer 4).

Power to Glorify Jesus

(43) This is the primary role of the Holy Spirit on earth—to glorify Jesus, as Jesus glorified his Father:

He will glorify me. (Jn 16:14)

(44) It was through the Holy Spirit that Jesus chose his apostles (Acts 1:2) and it is through them and through us his other chosen followers that glory will be given to Jesus. The Spirit gives us the power to bear witness to Jesus and proclaim him Lord of all creation in spite of persecution:

> *When the Advocate comes, whom I shall send to you from the Father, the Spirit of truth who issues from the Father, he will be my witness. And you too will be witnesses. . . .* (Jn 15:26-27)

(45) This is the power to let the world know we stand for Christ, the power to speak of him, to obey his commands even when it is difficult, to let others see us worship God, to bring others to him by our example. Perhaps you may not have used this power before; perhaps through lack of faith or courage you have somehow dishonored God's gift of his Spirit within you. Perhaps you often fail to be a witness for Christ when he so much wants to be heard and seen by the people with whom you associate.

It may help to recall the words of Jesus:

> *So if anyone declares himself for me in the presence of men, I will declare myself for him in the presence of my Father in heaven. But the one who disowns me in the presence of men, I will disown in the presence of my Father in heaven.* (Mt 10:32-33)

If God through his Spirit is present *for* us, we too must be present *for* him no matter where we are or what company we are in.

Power to Know the Truth

(46) Jesus is guiding his Church because his Spirit is "the
      Spirit of truth" (Jn 14:16) and he has told us that this
Spirit will remind us of all that he has said.

> *The Advocate, the Holy Spirit, who . . . will teach you
> everything. . . . (Jn 14:26)*

He is continually teaching each individual Christian who is
willing to listen, teaching you and me if we are childlike
of heart. He will not allow us to make wrong decisions if
we use the gift of wisdom which he has given us. If we
learn to rely on him and not on ourselves he will never fail
us whether it be in a choice of vocation, a difficult moral
decision or what prayers we should offer. Similarly, he will
help us in our ordinary decisions of daily life such as
buying a house, choosing a job, marrying a partner, having
children and in any other way.

(47) A person who is truly a Christian no longer relies on
      human wisdom:

> *I shall destroy the wisdom of the wise and bring to
> nothing all the learning of the learned. . . . Do you not
> see God has shown up the foolishness of human
> wisdom? (1 Cor 1:19-20)*

Power to Serve the Community

(48)
> *There is a variety of gifts but always the same Spirit.
> (1 Cor 12:4)*

A gift is a power for service to the community of the

Church. It is a talent given you *for others*. St. Paul mentions some of them—preaching, instructing, intense faith, healing, miracles, prophesying, recognizing spirits, being an apostle, a leader, a teacher, a helper, an almsgiver, speaking in tongues or interpreting tongues. He says—"all these are the work of the same Spirit, who distributes different gifts to different people just as he chooses" (1 Cor 12:11). These are gifts given to ordinary people like us. We may have one or more of them at different times. We may all very laudably pray for them with a readiness to accept them in humility as manifestations of God's power in us for the service of others.

(49) No one gets all the gifts. We each have to depend on the others in the Church. All these charismatic gifts are manifestations of Christ's power refracted like light into many colors for the building up of the Church. We must, of course, be careful to remember that these gifts are not of ourselves or from ourselves. They are simply God's power working *through* us. They are not necessarily permanent. It is always the right and the duty of our Church leaders to judge the genuineness and proper use of these gifts, and to see that when they are used "everything be done with propriety and order" (1 Cor 14:40).

Power to Live and Love as a Christian

(50) So the Christian life is not merely a *struggle* to do and to avoid. The Christian life is a *power* and a freedom to do and to avoid. The Holy Spirit is that power and freedom in us. We have the power to love and serve God even though our old and selfish nature is still alive. If we see life as a lonely effort to struggle against selfishness and sin, we are forgetting the great power within us; we are

like someone pushing a new gas-filled, well-oiled car
along because he has forgotten to switch it on. If we forget
this wonderful power that is in us, we are in danger of
growing very tired, and even giving up. Hear St. Paul:

> *Let me put it like this: if you are guided by the Spirit
> you will be in no danger of yielding to self-indulgence,
> since self-indulgence is the opposite of the Spirit . . .
> if you are led by the Spirit, no law can touch you. . . .
> (Here he mentioned the fruits of self-indulgence.)—
> What the Spirit brings is very different: love, joy,
> peace, patience, kindness, goodness, trustfulness,
> gentleness and self-control. . . . (Gal 5:16-24)*

He completes this with an appeal:

> *Since the Spirit is our life, let us be directed by the
> Spirit.* (Gal 5:25)

(51) It is not that we sit back and let the Holy Spirit make
us good or make us do the right thing; nor is it that
we exhaust ourselves trying to do the right thing and then
expect the Holy Spirit to come. Rather it is a matter of
recognizing our own helplessness in the struggle; then
calling on the power of the Holy Spirit already within us;
then stepping out confidently to do the right thing, knowing
that we are acting with the power of God. The fruits of the
Spirit enumerated above are already ours; we have only to
act in trust on the word of God. We have only to step out
in faith, believing that God is faithful and that he will honor
his promise.

(52) One of the surest signs that you are living a life of
faith in Jesus and with the power of the Holy Spirit is

the presence of peace in your heart and freedom from anxiety in what you are doing.

Power to Live the Life of Jesus

(53) By the full acceptance of his Spirit in us, we live the life of Jesus not our own life. This is not an achievement gained; it is more a gift accepted. It is as St. Paul says of himself to the Galatians:

> *The life I now live in this body I live by faith: faith in the Son of God who loved me and who sacrificed himself for my sake.* (Gal 2:20)

(54) If I do this I am bringing Christ forward into history which is still unwritten in my home, on my street, at my work, in my club, on the highway, golf course or where-ever.

Received at Baptism and Confirmation

(55) The power of the Holy Spirit expresses itself in many other ways, in every aspect of the Christian life. This great grace is given to us at baptism and confirmation. These sacraments are perfect and complete works of God alone but often they fail to have their full effect because of some obstacle in us. That obstacle may be lack of instruction, lack of faith, lack of maturity or lack of readiness to let go and give ourselves completely to God.

(56) It is for one of these reasons—not from any failure on God's part—that the experience of power, of fullness or victory did not come into our lives when we received these sacraments. The first Christians, because they were

prepared to renounce the world of sin completely, because
they were prepared to "burn their boats" and to cease being
"men of their time" had the experience of being transformed by the power of the Holy Spirit in these sacraments.
They had a real conversion.

Bringing This Power Alive in Us

(57) Perhaps many of us adult Christians need to be converted, to have the second conversion about which
spiritual writers speak, so that we enjoy the feeling of power
and victory which should really be part of the normal
Christian life. One leading Catholic theologian, Karl
Rahner, says that because we now live in an anti-Christian
world which cannot support us in our Christian lives, we
cannot survive in the long run without an adult conversion,
a personal fundamental choice of faith and the Christian
life.

(58) Have you ever made this choice by a formal and
sincere renewal of your baptismal vows as an adult,
and by asking God to bring all the power and fullness of the
Holy Spirit alive in you?

(59) Many Catholics today are experiencing a new victory
and powerful presence of the Holy Spirit in their lives
when they have done this.

*So I say to you: Ask, and it will be given to you; . . .
What father among you would hand his son a stone
when he asked for bread? . . . If you then, who are evil,
know how to give your children what is good, how
much more will the heavenly Father give the Holy Spirit
to those who ask him!* (Lk 11:9-13)

(60) Our Lady is the perfect model of our Christian response. She was told by the angel of God—"The Holy Spirit will come upon you and the power of the Most High will cover you with its shadow" (Lk 1:35). This took place in her life not by any merits on her part but simply as a gift from God:

> *He has looked upon his lowly handmaid.* (Lk 1:48)

But she was prepared to receive it by being *empty*, i.e., totally detached. She reminded us that this is the necessary prerequisite for being filled with God:

> *The hungry he has filled with good things, the rich sent empty away.* (Lk 1:52)

If you are hungry for the presence and power of God in your life, acknowledge your own poverty and emptiness, then with faith ask for the release of the power of the Holy Spirit whom you received at baptism and confirmation and you too will be able to say:

> *My soul proclaims the greatness of the Lord and my spirit exults in God my savior.* (Lk 1:46)

With the Holy Spirit or Without Him

(61) The Eastern part of the Church has usually been more aware of the Holy Spirit than we of the West. In one of their books, *Dialogues with Patriarch Athenagoras,* we read this splendid summary of the importance of the Holy Spirit.

They are words which should be prayed over:

> *Without the Holy Spirit: God is far away,*

Christ stays in the past,
the gospel is a dead letter,
the Church is simply an organization,
authority a matter of domination,
mission a matter of propaganda,
the liturgy no more than an evocation,
Christian living a slave morality.
But in the Holy Spirit:
the cosmos is resurrected and groans with the
birthpangs of the Kingdom,
the risen Christ is there,
the gospel is the power of life,
the Church shows forth the life of the Trinity,
authority is a liberating service,
mission is a Pentecost,
the liturgy is both memorial and anticipation,
human action is deified.

Two Prayers:

(62) Each Pentecost, the official prayer of the Church is:

> *O God, by the mystery of today's feast, you*
> *bless your Church in every race and nation. Pour*
> *down upon the whole wide world the gifts of the*
> *Holy Spirit, and in our day inspire the hearts of the*
> *faithful to perform those selfsame works which by*
> *divine condescension were wrought when the*
> *gospel was first preached.*

Pope John XXIII gave us a similar prayer in preparation for the Second Vatican Council:

> *O Divine Spirit. . . . Renew your wonders in our time, as though for a new Pentecost, and grant that the Holy Church, preserving unanimous and continuous prayer, together with Mary, the mother of Jesus, and also under the guidance of St. Peter, may increase the reign of the Divine Savior, the reign of truth and justice, the reign of love and peace. Amen.*

We ought to say these prayers often.

POINTS FOR DISCUSSION

1. Give examples from the words of Jesus and the Acts of the Apostles to show that the Holy Spirit gives real spiritual power to all Christians.

2. What are charismatic gifts and why are they given?

3. How can a Christian best bring the power of the Holy Spirit alive within himself or herself?

4. What would you consider to be a formal and sincere renewal of your baptismal vows? How exactly do you think such a renewal ought to be made?

REVIEW

1. The Christian life is more an experience of receiving than giving.   T   F

2. Without receiving the Holy Spirit it is impossible to be a full Christian.   T   F

3. Jesus' work was complete when he ascended into heaven.   T   F

4. The Holy Spirit in our lives is an experience of power.   T   F

5. Jesus left his apostles for their own good.   T   F

6. Christ's risen body now gives unending life to the Christian.   T   F

7. Jesus now lives in heaven and in our tabernacles.   T   F

8. The word "advocate" means someone who is to judge us.   T   F

9. Knowing God is the same as knowing about him.   T   F

10. St. Peter changed because he received a new power into his life.   T   F

11. By faith and baptism we have the power of God in us if we use it.   T   F

12. A Christian can no longer live for himself
    alone.   T   F

13. It is with his own effort and his own love
    that a Christian loves God and others.   T   F

14. The primary role of the Holy Spirit is to
    glorify Jesus.   T   F

15. The gifts of the Spirit are to help one grow
    in holiness.   T   F

16. Ordinary people should not ask for the
    gifts of the Spirit.   T   F

17. The charismatic gifts are for all Christians. T   F

18. The power of God will remain dead in us
    unless we use it.   T   F

19. A Christian can bring Christ forward into
    history.   T   F

20. Lack of instruction, of faith or readiness
    to let go limits God's power in us.   T   F

21. Every Christian adult should make a deep
    act of faith in Jesus at some time.   T   F

22. Hunger for God is a condition of receiving
    him.   T   F

23. Pentecost was a once-for-all event in the
    Church.   T   F

Chapter 5

LET US PRAY

(1) By prayer we express friendship with God. It is much more a matter of the heart than of the head. It is helpful to reflect at times on the meaning of prayer, but it is much more important to pray. In this chapter we shall reflect upon some aspects of prayer, but we do this only to help you pray better. You may already be praying very well, but we hope that this chapter will give you a deeper love for prayer and deeper peace and joy in it.

May Jesus live by faith in the heart of every reader of this chapter. May he give you the power through his Spirit to grow strong in faith and hope and love.

(2) Prayer is very personal. No two people pray exactly alike. Each one of us shows his or her love for friends in a unique way. So, in this chapter, it would not be possible—and even if it were it would be unwise—to give you detailed directions about how you should express your own personal prayers. Your style of prayer, the amount of time you need to pray, and the words you use cannot be legislated by anyone; they are uniquely yours and entirely your own responsibility.

What Is Prayer?

(3)   In the chapter on "Living Faith" we described faith
        as a posture of heart or an attitude before God, our
heavenly Father. This posture of heart includes recognition
of God's greatness, goodness, power and mercy with our
whole person. When we have this recognition of God in
our hearts we love him. When we show this love we are
praying. We show it either by thinking of him lovingly, by
our words, by our gestures, or by doing what we know he
asks of us. In each case we are expressing our faith, and
so we are praying. We are sincerely giving God signs that
we love him.

Jesus Praying in Us

(4)   We can never understand prayer fully because it is an
        entering into the inner life of God, and a sharing in
that life. However, the things God has revealed to us about
his own inner life help us to understand many things about
prayer. God's greatest revelation to us is the Blessed
Trinity; the knowledge that within the inner life of God
there are three distinct persons, the Father, the Son, and
the Spirit. This is a divine community of love within God
himself. God *is* a community of love.

When the Second Person of the Blessed Trinity became
man he made it possible for us to share in the love community life of God. That act of sharing in the life of God
is at the very heart of prayer.

(5)   In the community of God (the Blessed Trinity) the
        Son has always offered perfect prayer of praise and
worship to the Father. By his Holy Spirit, he lives now in

us his people. So by the same Holy Spirit he continues to pray in us. He gives us the privilege of sharing his movement of love toward the Father:

The proof that you are sons is that God has sent the Spirit of his Son into our hearts: the Spirit that cries, "Abba, Father." (Gal 4:6)

(6)   This cry of "Father" being spoken continually by the Spirit of Jesus through us is the heart of Christian prayer. All our prayers, if they are to be of true value, must be small streams entering this great river of worship between the Spirit-filled Church and the Father. St. Paul puts it this way:

No one can say, "Jesus is Lord" unless he is under the influence of the Holy Spirit. (1 Cor 12:3)

That is why St. Jude reminds us that we must be always:

praying in the Holy Spirit. (Jude 20)

Our prayer must be the prayer of the Spirit of Jesus, or it is not Christian prayer at all.

Christian Prayer Is Different

(7)   Christian prayer is different from all other prayer; it is not prayer to a God who is far away. It is, in a very true although mysterious way, a sharing in Jesus' prayer to the Father. So much so that at times when we don't know how best to pray or what words to use, we need not worry about it. This because:

The Spirit too comes to help us in our weakness. For when we cannot choose words in order to pray properly, the Spirit himself expresses our plea in a way

*that could never be put into words, and God who
knows everything in our hearts knows perfectly well
what he means, and that the pleas of the saints
(i.e., us) expressed by the Spirit are according to the
mind of God.* (Rom 8:26-27)

(8)   The more we are living in the Spirit the more effective
      our prayer is. The depth of our prayer depends on the
depth of our relationship with Jesus. It is living in the
Spirit which makes us fit to pray fully in the Spirit. To the
extent that we abide in Christ, to that extent we can ask the
Father anything in his name and receive it. If our lives
become really Christlike the wonderfully unlimited promises of Jesus will no longer appear strange. In each of our
prayers we will give the Father all honor and glory:

*With him (Jesus), through him and in him in the unity
of the Holy Spirit.*

(9)   We are not praying with our own weak and wayward
      love. By faith it is important to recall often that:

*The love of God has been poured into our hearts by the
Holy Spirit which has been given to us.* (Rom 5:5)

But love expresses itself in many ways. So our prayer is
very free to express whatever sentiment we wish and whenever we wish.

The Prayer of Praising Love

(10) The best prayer we can offer is to praise God. Praise
      of God is one of the chief reasons why we offer the
sacrifice of the Mass. In the fourth Eucharistic Prayer, immediately after the consecration, we pray for the Church:

By your Holy Spirit, gather all who share this one bread and one cup into the one body of Christ, a living sacrifice of praise.

We commence the third Eucharistic Prayer in these words:

Father, you are holy indeed, and all creation rightly gives you praise.

In almost every Mass we praise God together in that ancient Christian hymn:

Glory to God in the highest . . . we praise you for your glory.

How ought we express our prayers of praise? Many of the psalms can help us in that area. Psalm 150 is a good sample. We can pray right now.

Alleluia! (This means "Praise the Lord.")

Praise God in his Temple on earth,
praise him in his temple in heaven
praise him for his mighty achievements,
praise him for his transcendent greatness!
Praise him with blasts of the trumpet,
praise him with lyre and harp,
praise him with drums and dancing,
praise him with strings and reeds,
praise him with clashing cymbals,
praise him with clanging cymbals!
Let everything that breathes praise Yahweh!

                                               Alleluia!

For other examples of prayers of praise see Psalms 19, 47, 93, 95, 96, 100, 103, 135, 145, 148.

The Prayer of Grateful Love

(12) In heaven, as we say in the fourth Eucharistic Prayer:

> *We shall sing your glory with every creature through Christ our Lord, through whom you give us everything that is good.*

For this we must have a permanently grateful heart as St. Paul reminds us:

> *For all things give thanks to God because this is what God expects you to do in Christ Jesus.* (1 Thes 5:18)

We have so much to be grateful for especially for being sons and daughters of God. That is why we pray so frequently:

> *We come to you, Father, with praise and thanksgiving through Jesus Christ your Son.* (Eucharistic Prayer 1)

(13) After praising God, we cannot offer a better prayer than that of thanking him. The best thanks of all is the Eucharist lovingly offered and received. The word "eucharist" itself means *thanksgiving.* Having the living Christ within us we have the opportunity for perfect union with him in thanking the Father for his infinite goodness.

(14) Many find the psalms very helpful as prayers of thanksgiving. Psalm 138 is a delightful example. Read it prayerfully.

I thank you, Yahweh, with all my heart,
because you have heard what I said.
In the presence of the angels I play for you,
and bow down toward your holy Temple.

I give thanks to your name for your love and faith-
fulness;
your promise is even greater than your fame.
The day I called for help, you heard me
and you increased my strength.

Yahweh, all kings on earth give thanks to you,
for they have heard your promises;
they celebrate Yahweh's actions,
"Great is the glory of Yahweh!"
From far above, Yahweh sees the humble,
from far away he marks down the arrogant.

Though I live surrounded by trouble,
you keep me alive — to my enemies' fury!
You stretch your hand out and save me,
your right hand will do everything for me.
Yahweh, your love is everlasting,
do not abandon us whom you have made.

Other beautiful psalms of thanksgiving include Nos. 33, 40, 65, 66, 116, 136.

The Prayer of Trusting Love

(15) We trust those we love even when we cannot fully understand what they are doing. We accept them and so we accept what they do. A child will jump from a height into his father's arms without any guarantee that his father will catch him—he just trusts. A secure child will submit

to surgery if his loving parents assure him it is necessary.
Our heavenly Father often asks us too to trust him even
when we cannot understand what he is doing. He often
says "wait" but he never says "worry."

(16) Sometimes he asks us to jump, to step out of the boat
      like St. Peter, trusting him. At other times he sends
us trials to test our trust and to make it grow. When we
have perfect trust in God, then our faith is complete. St.
James expresses it this way:

> My brothers, you will always have your trials, but when
> they come, try to treat them as a happy privilege; you
> understand that your faith is only put to the test to
> make you patient; but patience too is to have its prac-
> tical results so that you will become fully developed,
> complete, with nothing missing. (Jas 1:2-4)

When we pray in suffering asking God to heal us, this
is an excellent prayer, but he may inspire us to pray the
prayer of patience and trust instead. The well-known Good
Shepherd psalm is a splendid example:

> The Lord is my shepherd,
> I lack nothing. . . . (Ps 23:1)

Psalms 26, 27, 31, 46, 55, 62, 127, 131 are more very
helpful prayers of trusting love.

The Prayer of Repentant Love

(17) We have seen the fundamental importance of this in
      the chapter entitled "Turning to God." Every day we
ask forgiveness for our trespasses because we know that

in some way we have failed to live up to God's great love for us. We are sinful and we have sinned. This prayer of repentant love can be expressed in an act of contrition, by penance freely chosen in reparation to the Sacred Heart of Jesus, and most of all in the personal encounter with Jesus in the sacrament of his mercy.

(18) We also offer this prayer when we forgive others their faults against us. The Holy Spirit enables us to forgive others. The greater our sins in the sight of God, the greater has been his forgiveness. In this we may claim a special kinship with Mary Magdalen of whom Jesus said:

> *I tell you that her sins, her many sins, must be forgiven her, or she would not have shown such great love.*
> *It is the man who is forgiven little who shows little love.* (Lk 7:47)

It is in this way that our sinfulness can become a source for praying the prayer of repentant love every day. Chapter two quoted King David's beautiful psalm of repentance, Psalm 51. Psalms 6 and 32 also are prayers of repentance.

The Prayer of Intercessory Love

Jesus gives us this great promise:

> *If you remain in me and my words remain in you, you will ask what you will and you shall get it.* (Jn 15:7)

The promise is clear and has only one condition attached to it—that we remain in his love. He tells us how we do this:

> *If you keep my commandments you will remain in my love.* (Jn 15:10)

(20) It simply states that Father-like giving will always be a response to childlike living. The Father giving and the child receiving belong to each other. The secret of effective prayer is a heart filled with love of the Father, a heart that says and means *"Abba,* Father."

(21) If we remain in his love by having a Christlike posture of heart and living a Christlike life, then we are sure that we will be inspired to ask for the things which best promote God's glory and we are sure of receiving them. This receiving adds to God's glory:

> *Whatever you ask for in my name I will do, so that the Father may be glorified in the Son.* (Jn 14:13)

We can ask for anything—even our own success, as Jesus did—provided it is ultimately for God's glory:

> *Father . . . glorify your Son so that your Son may glorify you.* (Jn 17:1)

(22) Before we pray for a request we must seek the Holy Spirit to enlighten us if we should ask at all. If we listen, he will not leave us in doubt. He may point out to us that either we are not praying properly or praying out of selfishness as St. James reminds us:

> *Why you don't have what you want is because you don't pray for it; when you do pray and don't get it, it is because you have not prayed properly; you have prayed for something to indulge your own desires.* (Jas 4:2-3)

(23) When what we ask is clearly God's will, we must ask with great boldness as Jesus did in all his prayers:

I know indeed that you always hear me. (Jn 11:42)

We must imitate him whenever we are not sure that what we ask is according to his will:

Nevertheless, let it be as you not I, would have it. (Mt 26:39)

(24) Otherwise we ought to persevere with complete confidence that our prayer will certainly be answered. The example of the Canaanite woman (Mt 15:21-28), of the importunate friend (Lk 11:5-8), and of the widow who persevered (Lk 18:1-8) are for our imitation.

(25) And there is so much to pray for—the coming of God's kingdom in men's hearts, the growth in love of God's Church, the unity of that Church, our national leaders, the homeless and the hungry of the world, the sick and lonely we know, our church leaders, the missionaries who represent us, our children's teachers, our family, our friends, our own health and happiness, and the many things we need each day.

Pray all the time, asking for what you need, praying in the Spirit on every possible occasion. Never get tired of staying awake to pray for all the saints. (Eph 6:18)

(26) In his sermon on the mount (*his policy speech*) Jesus gave us a beautiful picture of the power of intercessory prayer.

Is there a man among you who would hand his son a stone when he asked for bread? Or would hand him a snake when he asked for a fish? If you, then, who are evil, know how to give your children what is good, how much more will your Father in heaven give good things to those who ask him!" (Mt 7:9-11)

The Prayers of the Saints

(27) The scriptures are full of people who made intercession for others as Our Lady did at the wedding
feast, or as St. Paul did when he wrote to the Christians
at Ephesus:

I . . . have never failed to remember you in my prayers and to thank God for you. (Eph 1:16)

Moses held up his hands in prayer for the original people
of God.

(28) In the Christian community we pray for one another
especially when someone asks us for prayers. But the
Christian community transcends death; it extends beyond
this life into eternity. After death all the faithful are still
members of God's people, still part of Christ's body. We
still "belong to each other" (Rom 12:5). That is why we
have absolute faith that we still enjoy the prayer support
of "Mary, the virgin mother of God; with the apostles, the
martyrs and all the saints, on whose constant intercession
we rely for help" (Eucharistic Prayer 3). We invoke their
prayerful intercession with confidence.

Sincerity in Prayer

(29) Prayer is the privilege of making direct contact with
the heart of our loving heavenly Father. Jesus once
said:

In your prayers do not babble as the pagans do, for they think that by using many words they will make themselves heard. (Mt 6:7)

God weighs our prayers rather than counts them. Jesus gave us the perfect prayer:

Our Father in heaven,
may your name be held holy,
your kingdom come,
your will be done,
on earth as in heaven.
Give us today our daily bread.
And forgive us our debts,
as we have forgiven those who are in debt to us.
And do not put us to the test,
but save us from the evil one. (Mt 6:10-13)

It is only when we can say this slowly and with deep sincerity that other prayers will have meaning and value for us.

(30) Our prayers, just like any other meeting with a friend, call for privacy at most times and so Jesus told us:

When you pray, go to your private room and when you shut your door, pray to your Father in that secret place. (Mt 6:5)

Normally we cannot afford to leave the time and place of prayer to chance if we are serious about this central activity of the Christian life. Jesus weighs our prayers in yet another way:

And when you stand in prayer, forgive whatever you have against anybody. (Mk 11:25)

Without this we are pretending to love our Father while we are not prepared to forgive our brothers and sisters, his other children whom he loves so much. He will give us

the power to forgive anyone anything because he com-
manded it and he stressed that without it prayer is counter-
feit. Ask the Holy Spirit to give you the power to forgive
your enemies.

Expressing Our Prayers

(31) It is normal to use gestures in prayer but when we do
so it is important that these gestures be helpful to us
personally. There are some accepted gestures with which
people *pray together.* The Church has given us a combi-
nation of words and gestures to use in our public worship or
liturgy. The priest at Mass usually prays with his hands
raised; he kisses the gospel; he bows before the crucifix,
etc. These are prayers in gesture. We all pray in gesture
when we genuflect, bless ourselves, and strike our breasts or
bow our heads. These gestures are prayers if they come
from a true posture of heart. For instance, St. Paul wrote
with this suggestion:

*In every place, then, I want the men to lift their hands
up reverently in prayer.* (1 Tm 2:8)

(32) When you pray *privately* in your own room, or before
the Blessed Sacrament, you may like to just sit and
think lovingly of God, to read his word in the scriptures and
speak to him about it, to kneel and say some prayers which
you know by heart, to stand with your hands extended as
the priest does during Mass, or to sing a hymn in praise of
God. You may even like to cry before God. At another
time you may wish to walk around while you say a decade
of the rosary or pray a few psalms which express how you
feel toward God at that moment. It does not matter how
your prayers are expressed so long as they come from your
heart, and so long as your prayers are not mere empty

words or meaningless gestures. Jesus condemned any show
of prayer which was not sincere.

*This people honors me only with lip service, while their
hearts are far from me. The worship they offer me is
worthless.* (Mt 15:8-9)

(33) Each of us must gradually find his or her *own style
in prayer.* We should feel free to change it when a
new style will help us pray better. At one time we may feel
like singing a hymn of joy or repentance; at another time
it may help us more to be silent as we think over God's love
for us. At another, it may be that we feel like reading our
favorite prayer slowly over and over again. There are times
when we will like to kneel, at others to stand, at others
to bow, to raise our hands, or even to dance in the presence
of God. All of these have been used by men and women
of God, the saints of the Old and New Testaments. We
read about Jesus:

*And going on a little further, he fell on his face and
prayed.* (Mt 26:39)

and

*David danced whirling round before the Lord with all
his might.* (2 Sm 6:14)

(34) Prayer is also expressed by *fasting* as well as by words
and gestures. This is sometimes necessary, especially
when the devil seems to have more power in our lives or in
the lives of others. The Church still exhorts us to fast even
though detailed laws are not made about it. Jesus himself
gave us the example of this:

He fasted for forty days and forty nights. (Mt 4:2)

Similarly the *giving of alms* to the poor is an expression
of prayer:

> *Set aside part of your goods for almsgiving. Never
> turn your face from any poor man and God will never
> turn his from you. Measure your alms by what you
> have; if you have much, give more; if you have little,
> give less, but do not be mean in giving alms. By doing
> so, you will lay up for yourself a great treasure for the
> day of necessity. For almsgiving delivers from death
> and saves men from passing down to darkness. Alms
> is a most effective offering for all those who give it in
> the presence of the Most High.* (Tb 4:7-12)

When Do We Pray?

(35) If one of your children asks you — "Mommy/Daddy
     when should I love you?" — the answer is obvious. St.
Paul says:

> *Pray all the time.* (Eph 6:18)

and

> *Pray constantly.* (1 Thes 5:17)

This does not mean that we must be always thinking about
God or speaking to God. If our posture of heart is right
we are in a sense praying all the time in everything we do,
just as a man who really loves his wife is loving her when
he is working for a livelihood. That is why it is important
to obey the word of God in this way:

> *Whatever you eat, whatever you drink, whatever you do
> at all, do it for the glory of God.* (1 Cor 10:31)

(36) But at the same time, it is vital that we put aside spe-
     cial times for more direct and more intensive prayer.

A man and his wife, while they love each other all the time even when apart, must find time to be alone for special and deeper expressions of their love for each other. So also with our love for God; at times we must be alone with him.

The simple practice of *morning and evening prayer* cannot be too highly recommended. Jesus himself used both times for prayer:

> *In the morning long before dawn, he got up and left the house, and went off to a lonely place and prayed there.* (Mk 1:35)

and

> *After saying good-bye to them he went off into the hills to pray. When evening came, the boat was on the lake, and he was alone on the land.* (Mk 6:46-47)

(37) There are special times when we need to hear God's voice more clearly or when we want some special help for ourselves or others. When Jesus was about to make the serious decision about the choice of his apostles, we read:

> *Now it was about this time that he went out into the hills to pray; and he spent the whole night in prayer to God. When day came he summoned his disciples and picked out twelve of them.* (Lk 6:12-13)

This is an example for us to follow at special times when we have *big decisions* ahead of us. Do we sincerely pray about the decisions we are asked to make?

(38) In time of temptation, when the devil seems to be particularly near us, we must do what Jesus told his apostles:

You should be awake and praying not to be put to the test. (Mt 26:41)

Prayer Together

(39) We shall see in our chapter on the Christian community that the Church is the people of God, and that he wants us to worship him together as well as individually and alone. Our leaders in the Church have outlined how some of this prayer together should be offered, especially when we worship at Mass, when we approach Jesus in the sacraments, or when we pray in the name of the whole Church using the official "prayer of the Church." This beautifully arranged prayer is now available to everyone.

(40) Immediately after the ascension of Jesus into heaven we read about his followers:

These remained faithful . . . to the breaking of bread and to the prayers . . . . They went as a body to the Temple every day but met in their houses for the breaking of bread. (Acts 2:42, 46)

But we don't have to wait for our weekly and official worship in order to pray together. Jesus said:

Where two or three meet in my name, I shall be there with them. (Mt 18:20)

(41) So when we are in the company of one other Christian, it is good to pray together because Jesus is present with us in a special way. He is praying with us in a unique way when we stand beside another person and we pray together. The simple practice of family prayer ensures the presence of Jesus in your family.

I tell you solemnly once again, if two of you on earth

*agree to ask anything at all, it will be granted to you
by my Father in heaven.* (Mt 18:19)

In the next chapter we will refer more fully to the value
of small praying communities of three or four families. Can
you meet for private prayer with other families?

The Experience of Prayer

(42) These verses of Psalm 139 are deep prayer. If said
after calling on the Holy Spirit who guided the author
in writing it, they will give you the perfect prayer-posture
before God. Ponder each line in your heart before pro-
ceeding to the next one.

*Yahweh, you examine me and know me,
you know if I am standing or sitting,
you read my thoughts from far away,
whether I walk or lie down, you are watching,
you know every detail of my conduct.*

*The word is not even on my tongue,
Yahweh, before you know all about it;
close behind and close in front you fence me around,
shielding me with your hand.
Such knowledge is beyond my understanding,
a height to which my mind cannot attain.*

*Where could I go to escape your Spirit?
Where could I flee from your presence?
If I climb the heavens, you are there,
there too, if I lie in the Sheol.*

If I flew to the point of sunrise,

or westward across the sea,
your hand would still be guiding me,
your right hand holding me.

If I asked darkness to cover me,
and light to become night around me,
that darkness would not be dark to you,
night would be as light as day.

It was you who created my inmost self,
and put me together in my mother's womb;
for all these mysteries I thank you:
for the wonder of myself, for the wonder of your works.

You know me through and through
from having watched my bones take shape
when I was being formed in secret,
knitted together in the limbo of the womb.

You had scrutinized my every action,
all were recorded in your book,
my days listed and determined,
even before the first of them occurred.

God, how hard it is to grasp your thoughts!
How impossible to count them!
I could no more count them than I could the sand,
and suppose I could, you would still be with me.

God, examine me and know my heart,
probe me and know my thoughts;
make sure I do not follow pernicious ways,
and guide me in the way that is everlasting. (Ps 139:1-
　　18, 23-24)

By prayer we draw on the infinite resources of the divine power; we open our hearts to God; we make ourselves available to him so that he can speak to us and through us.

One prayerful young man writes of his prayer life in these words:

> Sometimes I pray because it seems the right thing to do at that particular time; sometimes because I feel the presence of Christ in me. Other times I pray because I do not feel Christ at all, but want to. I may find him in myself, in my neighbor, in the physical world or in himself through the Eucharist. He is present in all these forms; it is for me to seek out and be open to these possibilities. We will not know God by means of ideas as much as through openness and love.

> The more we pray, the more we bring Christ to ourselves. And by bringing Christ to ourselves we are bringing him to others through our contact with them. As others pray they will bring Christ indirectly to us. Each time we pray we renew our openness to Christ, and we continue in our growing love for him.

A Prayer to Jesus

Lord Jesus, teach me how to pray. You alone can teach me as you taught your apostles. I sincerely wish to pray well and to grow in friendship with you, but I do not know how to pray as I ought.

Lord give me a deep sense of the need that is in me to remain quietly in your presence long enough to hear what you are saying to me. Convince me deeply of the power of prayer and of the truth that it is your Spirit within me that will make my prayers powerful.

Lord give me an expectant faith. Fill me with confidence that with you as my teacher I can really learn to pray well in spite of my own nothingness. Let me be convinced that you will reveal to me all I need to know in order to pray well. Give me such deep confidence in the power of prayer that I will welcome opportunities to pray for others. Take away all human respect so that I may stand joyfully beside all who ask me for prayers and speak out the words of prayer to you in their presence. Let me grow ever more aware that you Lord Jesus are alive in me, and that all my prayers are full of power for good because they are your prayers spoken through me.

POINTS FOR DISCUSSION

1. In prayer we do not merely talk to God; we enter into his own community of love. What does this mean?

2. Give some reasons why the prayer of praise is said to be the greatest prayer of all?

3. Quote some of the things Jesus said about prayer, and give your favorite passage from his words about prayers of *petition*?

4. Give some reasons for the teachings of Jesus to show the special value of shared prayer. What do you think of shared *spontaneous* prayer?

R E V I E W

1. It is more important to understand
   prayer than to pray.   T   F

2. Nobody may tell me what words I
   should use in my prayers.   T   F

3. The revelation of the Blessed Trinity
   helps us to understand prayer.   T   F

4. The heart of Christian prayer is the cry
   of "Father" being spoken by the
   Holy Spirit through us.   T   F

5. We cannot pray if we do not know
   what words to use.   T   F

6. The depth of our prayer depends on
   our ability to speak spontaneously.   T   F

7. The best prayer we can offer is the
   prayer of praise.   T   F

8. God will not ask us to trust him if we
   cannot understand what he is doing to us.   T   F

9. Prayer of repentance is best expressed
   in the sacrament of Penance.   T   F

10. The most important requirement of
    prayer of petition is to keep on asking.   T   F

11. The secret of effective prayer is a
    heart filled with love for the Father.   T   F

12. If we listen to the Holy Spirit he will
tell us what to ask for in prayer.   T   F

13. In his Sermon on the Mount Jesus
compared his Father to the most
loving human father.   T   F

14. The scriptures tell us nothing about
the intercession of the saints.   T   F

15. The Christian community ends with death.   T   F

16. God weighs our prayers rather than
counts them.   T   F

17. If we have a prayerful heart we do not
need a special time for prayer.   T   F

18. Prayers in gestures are not as valuable
as prayers in words.   T   F

19. It is important to stick to the same
style of prayer all our lives.   T   F

20. Almsgiving is a prayer.   T   F

21. Special prayer is necessary before
making serious decisions.   T   F

22. Our prayers are best when we are alone.   T   F

23. Reading the psalms helps us to grow
in a spirit of prayer.   T   F

Chapter 6

THE CHRISTIAN COMMUNITY

(1)   Everyone wants to belong. No man is an island. We are all part of the mainland of humanity and we never cease wanting to belong to some group of friends. Loneliness is probably the hardest thing which the human heart has to suffer. People need people. Each of us needs others.

(2)   We were born into a family and that family belonged to a larger family of relatives. We then belong to a certain town or suburb. Maybe we belong to a certain city and of course to a country we call ours as well. None of this is by chance because it is built into man to congregate and to become a community with his fellowmen in so many ways.

(3)   Indeed we become fully human only through and with others. Unless we have friends we will never know what friendship means. Unless we encounter other persons we will never know what it means to be a person. Unless we live close to other people we never quite become fully human. This is a law built into our nature by God from the beginning:

It is not good that the man should be alone. (Gen 2:18)

(4)   For each one of us then to *be* is to *be with* others, to exist is to coexist with others. Man was born into a community, grows in community and it is also God's plan that we approach him in community.

God Chose a People

(5)   When God decided to choose the people who would form his church in the Old Testament, he spoke to a wandering desert tribe. According to the Hebrew way of thinking, the people form a whole and the individual is involved in the destiny of the whole. They had a deep sense of belonging. And when he chose Abraham he promised:

I will make you a great nation. (Gen 12:2)

(6)   This great nation promised by God to Abraham was to become God's church, God's chosen community of the Old Testament. This is when "God first arranged to enlist a people for his name from out of the pagans," as James told his fellow countrymen at Antioch. (Acts 15:14)

(7)   Later on God spoke to Moses and renewed his promise, his covenant to his chosen community:

I will adopt you as my own people, and I will be your God. (Ex 6:6)

and

If you obey my voice and hold fast to my covenant, you of all the nations shall be my very own for all the earth is mine. I will count you a kingdom of priests, a consecrated nation. (Ex 19:5-6)

(8)   On behalf of the community, Moses took sacrificial

blood, cast it over the people and said:

We will observe all that Yahweh has decreed; we will obey. This is the blood of the covenant that Yahweh has made with you containing all these rules. (Ex 24:7-8)

Because He Loved Them

(9) When Moses was calling for loyalty from the community, he reminded them that it was God's love which made them what they are; he let them know that their status was God's loving choice and not due to any merits on their part. He said:

For you are a people consecrated to Yahweh your God; it is you that Yahweh our God has chosen to be his very own people out of all the peoples on the earth. If Yahweh set his heart on you and chose you, it was not because you outnumbered other peoples; you were the least of all peoples. It was his love for you and to keep the oath he swore to your fathers. . . . (Deut 7:6-8)

(10) They were a small nation and in constant danger of being crushed nationally and religiously by big powers. But God told them that he was their king but a king who loved them and would always rescue them if they remained faithful to the covenant ratified when Moses poured out the sacrificial blood. Later on, when the people were not faithful to God's laws and forgot his love, he spoke through the prophet Hosea and said he loved them as a husband loved his wife:

That is why I am going to lure her and lead her out into the wilderness and speak to her heart . . . . When that day comes—it is Yahweh who speaks—she will call me, "My husband." (Hos 2:16, 18)

God's New People — the Church

(11)
We are those people; whether we were Jews or pagans we are the ones he has called. (Rom 9:24)

God's first chosen people were meant to worship him and to be a light to all other nations. This was their primary vocation. Through his Son, Jesus, he has now chosen others to be his people as we see in St. Paul's words above. He also wrote to the Corinthians:

Greetings to the church of God in Corinth, to the holy people of Jesus Christ. (1 Cor 1:2)

(12) The phrase "people of God" once reserved for the Jewish people alone, is now applied to the peoples of all nations who confess that Jesus is the Lord. This is the Church of which we are members; we are God's chosen community. We belong to the people of God by our faith in Jesus and by our baptism.*

---

*Without in any way sacrificing our traditional understanding of the Catholic Church as the one, true Church, we Catholics no longer think of membership in the true Church as simply existing or not existing. Since Vatican II we think in terms of *degrees* of membership. We see other Christians as being members of the true Church to whatever degree they share our faith and our sacraments. Furthermore, since Vatican II we recognize that the Holy Spirit is at work in and through non-Catholic churches as such, and not merely in individual non-Catholics. This implies that, although the fullness of the means of salvation is found only in the Catholic Church, other churches can witness to aspects of Christianity that have grown dim in the Catholic Church, and can therefore contribute to our spiritual enrichment.

(13) The people of God, the chosen community which he
 loved and guided, were always homeless, sojourning
among strangers, forever on the move, a pilgrim people.
They knew that:

*God told them to leave their home and set out for
Canaan.* (Jdt 5:9)

We too as the new people of God, his New Testament
Church, must never forget that we too are not a settled but
a sojourning people, not permanently in one place but
pioneers on the way to heaven. As strangers and pilgrims,
we have not here a lasting city, but we seek the one that
is to come. "We wait in joyful hope for the coming of our
savior Jesus Christ" (Communion Rite).

A People With Power
(14)
 *You will receive power when the Holy Spirit comes on
 you, and then you will be my witnesses.* (Acts 1:8)

In these words Jesus reminds his followers that the
Church will not be a group of men worshiping the Father
and witnessing to him by *their own* power. He has brought
them together as a community and celebrated this at the
Last Supper, but during his final instruction he said to
them:

*Now I am sending down to you what the Father has
promised. Stay in the city then, until you are clothed
with power from on high.* (Lk 24:49)

(15) This new power which he had promised them on sev-
 eral occasions is the Holy Spirit, God's own dynamic

love. Without this they would be a group of well-intentioned but weak men, but with this supreme gift of God, they will be a people of God with *God's own* power in them. The Holy Spirit is thus the Church in the hearts of men. Everything else in the Church — the Eucharist, the laws, the pope and the bishops — is there at the service of this great transformation of men into Christ by the presence and power of his Holy Spirit.

The Power of God's Spirit

(16) At Pentecost Jesus came to live in his Church in a new way by the power of the Holy Spirit. The journey of the new people of God began at this moment of Pentecost and it will be completed only at the second coming of Jesus. At this moment too, his followers experienced a new reality in their lives. It was now at last that they fully believed Jesus was the Lord and understood the events they had lived through with him.

(17) They also experienced themselves as a community bound together in Christ and by the Holy Spirit. The parallel which St. Luke draws between the gift of tongues and the Tower of Babel is very significant. At Babel, through man's rejection of God, the human race is divided. At Pentecost men are reunited as a community into God's family through faith and the Holy Spirit. They are now joined by the new covenant written in their hearts rather than on tablets of stone. They are now called as a church, a community, into a real sonship and daughterhood with the Father, and to a new morality which is dominated by love.

(18) Just as the Spirit is the bond of unity between Father

and Son, so is he the bond uniting the Christian to Christ, to the Father and to other Christians. The prayer of Jesus at the Last Supper becomes a reality:

Father, may they be one in us, as you are in me and I am in you. (Jn 17:21)

The Holy Spirit is the principle and power behind this community.

It is the Holy Spirit too who makes the Church the sign and the means of salvation for all men. Without him it is just a group of men trying to live by some laws and follow Jesus by their own power. Without him the Church would be merely a human and sinful reality.

(19) It is also by the power of the Holy Spirit that the Church can give witness to Jesus:

When the Advocate comes, whom I shall send you from the Father, the Spirit of truth who issues from the Father, he will be my witness, and you too will be my witnesses. (Jn 15:26-27)

(20) Thus it is the Holy Spirit in the Church who enables us and others to hear and accept Jesus who is the Word of God. Jesus is the visible sign and revelation of God but he has to be recognized and accepted as such:

No one can say, "Jesus is the Lord" unless he is under the influence of the Holy Spirit. (1 Cor 12:3)

It was only after Pentecost that the disciples themselves knew and recognized Jesus as the Lord and were transformed into a believing community — the Church.

(21) The Holy Spirit fulfills much the same role in the life
     of the Church as he did in the life of Jesus. As he is
the love of God, it is through him that the Father acts to
make Christians of us at baptism and to make us grow as
Christians. It is by the presence of the Holy Spirit in us
that the Church becomes Christ living again and still doing
God's work of worship and of witness everywhere and to
the end of time.

The Church Is Christ

(22) Because the Holy Spirit is present in us through faith
     and the sacrament of baptism, Christ is living again
in us:

> *Just as the human body, though it is made up of many
> parts, is a single body, so it is with Christ. In one Spirit
> we were all baptized . . . .* (1 Cor 12:12)

On another occasion Paul says:

> *Now you together are Christ's body.* (1 Cor 12:27)

This is our great privilege as members of the Church — to
permit Jesus to live his life again in us, the members of his
people alive by the power of his Holy Spirit.

We Are the Church

(23) Speaking to his apostles after the Last Supper Jesus
     used the example of a tree to explain vividly to us that
we live by the same life, the life of God which comes to us
"by the working of the Holy Spirit" (Eucharistic Prayer 3).
Without our membership in Christ and his Church, we can
do nothing.

(24) Jesus told us at his Last Supper:

Make your home in me, as I make mine in you.
(Jn 15:4)

This *home* is the Church, the Christian community, the people of God who have repented, believed, have been baptized and received the Holy Spirit. In the Church we belong; in the Church we achieve what he asks of us, and it is only in the Church we become what he wants us to become in this life and in the next.

Different Parts of Christ

(25) It would be impossible for any one person to express or show forth the whole life of Jesus in the Church. So God gives different gifts, different ministries and vocations to each person.

Now you together are Christ's body, but each of you is a different part of it. (1 Cor 12:27)

Some gifts he gives permanently and some for a time. But every gift is for the whole body; it is to serve Jesus in others; it is never for oneself alone.

There is a variety of gifts but always the same Spirit; there are all sorts of service to be done, but always to the same Lord; working in all sorts of different ways in different people, it is the same God who is working in all of them. The particular way in which the Spirit is given to each person is for a good purpose. (1 Cor 12:4-7)

(26) He then goes on to speak about the gifts and vocations — apostles, prophets, teachers, miracle workers, healing, helpers, leaders, those who speak with tongues, those who can interpret them, those who can recognize spirits, those who preach with wisdom, those who give instruction,

pastors and evangelists and those with extraordinary faith. These are all the work of the Holy Spirit given to each.

> *So that the saints* (i.e., we) *together make a unity in the work of service, building up the body of Christ. In this way we all are to come to unity in our faith and in our knowledge of the Son of God until we become the perfect man, fully mature with the fullness of Christ himself.* (Eph 4:12-13)

(27) So, you and I are in the Church to serve all its members, to build up the body of Christ by adding new members and by "helping each other to be better Christians."

A People Praising God

(28) In a letter of guidance to the people of God, Peter, the "rock" on which Christ built his Church, told us what we are and what our primary work in life as God's people is:

> *But you are a chosen race, a royal priesthood, a consecrated nation, a people set apart to sing the praises of God who called you out of darkness into his wonderful light.* (1 Pt 2:9)

(29) Worship by praise and thanksgiving is the first work of the people of God. Jesus worshiped his Father perfectly by his life, death and resurrection and he gave us the power to do the same:

> *Then he took some bread and when he had given thanks, broke it and gave it to them saying, "This is my body which will be given up for you; do this as a memorial of me." He did the same with the cup after*

supper, and said, "This cup is the new covenant in my blood which will be poured out for you." (Lk 22:19-20)

(30) This exactly is what we, the people of God, do each time we celebrate Mass. Through Jesus, with Jesus and in Jesus in the unity of the Holy Spirit, we offer God "all honor and glory." It is at this moment, if you are sincere in faith and obedience, that you are most a Christian in communion with God's people around his altar.

A People With Priorities

(31) After the coming of the Holy Spirit on the Church at Pentecost, the activity of the early Christian community is given us in these words:

These remained faithful to the teaching of the apostles, to the brotherhood, to the breaking of bread and to the prayers. (Acts 2:42)

(32) These also must be our priorities in the Church today. Are we faithful to these things before all else?

—*To the teaching of the Church?*
—*To love for each other?*
—*To Mass?*
—*To prayers?*

A People Loving One Another

(33)
By this love you have for one another, everyone will know that you are my disciples. (Jn 13:35)

The praise of God in the heart and on the lips of a Christian will flow over to his active love of others. As Jesus said in the words above, this will be the distinguishing mark of those who really are his disciples. He spent his life helping other people to be happy in this life and in the next. This is the life of a Christian too. St. Paul tells us that each of us is "a servant of the Church" (Col 1:25). It is not how much we know or what we know that makes us acceptable to God, but rather how much we love and how much we serve:

"We all have knowledge"; yes, that is so, but knowledge gives self-importance—it is love that makes the building grow. (1 Cor 8:1)

(34) Nor is it a matter of obeying a law about love; rather it is loving Jesus or failing to do so in the person beside us. It is on this we shall be judged in the end:

insofar as you did this to one of the least of these brothers of mine, you did it to me. (Mt 25:40)

And when Saul (who later became St. Paul) tried to hurt members of the Church, Jesus said to him:

I am Jesus, and you are persecuting me. (Acts 9:5)

(35) The Church is a community of people actively concerned for one another, really interested in one another, truly having time for one another, and loving one another deeply. If it is not that, it is not the Church as Jesus wants it to be. Each one of us makes it more or less the Church of Jesus when we love or fail to love, help or fail to help, pray for or fail to pray for others. And every act of love or failure to love, makes you more or less a member of Christ's Church.

(36) No matter what other gifts we have, if we do not have love we are useless. St. Paul told the Corinthians: "Without love, I am nothing at all" (1 Cor 13:2). He goes on to spell out what love means in everyday living:

*Love is always patient and kind; it is never jealous;
love is never boastful or conceited; it is never rude or
selfish; it does not take offense, and is not resentful.
Love takes no pleasure in other people's sins but
delights in the truth; it is always ready to excuse, to
trust, to hope, and to endure whatever comes; love does
not come to an end. . . . (1 Cor 13:4-7)*

(37) It is so important in the Christian community, that
God will not accept our gifts unless we love and forgive our neighbor:

*So then, if you are bringing your offering to the altar
and there remember that your brother has something
against you, leave your offering there before the altar,
go and be reconciled with your brother first and then
come back and present your offering. (Mt 5:23-24)*

(38) A Christian also loves and serves those who are members of the Church, or appear not to be members of it.
We shall look at this in another chapter.

A thought to ponder:

*How real is my membership in God's people when
measured against the quality of my concern and the
depth of my love for everyone in my parish?*

A People Being Taught

(39)
*The Church of the living God, which upholds truth and
keeps it safe. (1 Tm 3:15)*

This is what St. Paul said to Timothy just before he
mentioned "deceitful spirits and doctrines that come from
the devil." No one wants to be deceived, especially in im-

portant matters of life and death. We want to be sure that
we are right, especially in the important things. Here we
have the Word of God telling us that his Church upholds the
truth and keeps it safe. This, of course, is not because those
who lead the Church are wise men or because they know
theology. It is only because Jesus promised his Church:

> *But when the Spirit of truth comes he will lead you to
> the complete truth. . . . (Jn 16:13)*

(40) The Church will always be faithful to "the teaching of
the apostles" as was the first community of Christians.
We have Jesus' promise for this. The Holy Spirit is still with
the Church and leading it to the complete truth.

(41) Notice that the discovery of truth even for the Church
is not a sudden thing; the Church is being led, because
it is made up of human beings, to the complete truth. God
will see to it that the Church always has the truth necessary for the times. This is so because Jesus did not leave
a book of rules or a set of written beliefs which each one
would have to read and interpret for himself or herself. No,
he said:

> *Go therefore . . . and teach them. . . . (Mt 28:19-20)*

and he assured us:

> *I am with you always; yes, to the end of time. (Mt 28:20)*

(42) Jesus is alive in his Church guiding us to the truth.
Because of this the Church can never go wrong about
any fundamental teaching of Jesus. We should thank God
for this often, especially in a time when there is great confusion in the minds of so many people.

A People With Leaders

You are Peter and on this rock I will build my church.
(Mt 16:18)

(43) The Church is neither a dictatorship in which one man holds absolute power over all the others nor a democracy in which truth is arrived at by majority vote. It is a community of love in which we are taught by the Holy Spirit. He speaks through any of us as he chooses, even the most lowly. He breathes where he wills (cf. Jn 3:8).

(44) The whole community, acting through those to whom Jesus gives ministries of leadership within it, discerns whether or not any particular teaching is really from the Holy Spirit, or what exactly this or that particular teaching means for us. None of us may isolate ourselves from the community's teaching or from its leadership if we are to remain truly Christian. This is crucial.

(45) Jesus gave to one man, Peter, *the final say* in discerning divine truth and teaching it to the whole world. This ministry is shared primarily by *the twelve* and their successors, the pope and the bishops. It is shared in a subsidiary way by all to whom they delegate teaching ministries. All of us in the Church must listen to the guidance of our pope, our bishops, our pastors, and our religious teachers in order to learn divine truth. They in turn must listen to the community in order to hear and discern the living voice of the Holy Spirit. It is right that we would offer our leaders our vision of the truth as we see it after serious prayer and reflection. Pastoral councils on parochial and diocesan levels make practical provision for that.

The letter to the Hebrews says:

Obey your leaders and do as they tell you, because they must give an account of the way they look after your souls; make this a joy for them to do, and not a grief— you yourselves would be the losers. (Heb 13:17)

(46) In these days when the very notion of anyone being in authority is sometimes questioned, it is important that we recognize that there is authority in the Church founded by Jesus. The teaching leadership of the pope and bishops is obviously the result of the guidance of the Holy Spirit as Jesus promised:

The Advocate, the Holy Spirit, whom the Father will send in my name, will teach you everything and remind you of all I have said to you. (Jn 14:26)

(47) It is through the apostles and their successors that the Spirit preserves the unity of truth, worship and life in the Church.

In the first years of the Church St. Luke solemnly introduced a sermon by saying:

Then Peter stood up with the Eleven and addressed them. (Acts 2:14)

and

So the Twelve called a full meeting of the disciples and addressed them. (Acts 6:2)

(48) We are told Paul and Silas traveled, consolidating the local churches and that:

As they visited one town after another, they passed on the decisions reached by the apostles and elders in

Jerusalem, with instructions to respect them.
(Acts 16:4)

Thus the apostles and their successors are the sign of that unity of which the Holy Spirit is the source for the people of God.

The Church Which Is Your Parish

(49) Because close community is possible only in small numbers, the apostles founded churches as they went from town to town. There were churches at Corinth, at Ephesus and at Colossae, for instance, and each one had different people exercising the different gifts within it for the benefit of all. Each church had its leaders, teachers, preachers, prophets, pastors and healers.

(50) These churches could correspond to what we now call a parish. In strictly biblical terms the word "parish" means a group of people who are homeless or living alongside strangers or are resident aliens. It means a group of Christians living in a world to which they did not fully belong. They are the presence of Jesus among the pagans as he once again worships, witnesses, preaches, teaches, heals, and above all loves them even though he may be rejected by them.

(51) The parish is a number of people who love one another just as Jesus loves each of them. It is a group of people listening very reverently together with their pastor for the will of their Lord in their here-and-now situation. But, above all, a parish is a community of people who worship God together and each week celebrate their unity and their struggles together before the altar of God. They are

involved people, involved with one another but especially
with God through the Spirit of Jesus living in each by
baptism.

(52) This may sound like a rather distant ideal; nevertheless, it is what God wants his Church to be. The
parish is the Church in miniature and the life of the Church
will be just as healthy as the life of its parishes.

(53) The pastor is first of all a man who can say, like Jesus:

*I have come so that they may have life and have it to
the full. I am the good shepherd: the good shepherd is
one who lays down his life for his sheep. . . . I know my
own and my own know me.* (Jn 10:10-14)

He is offering his life for God's people in this parish and
because he is "dedicated to God" in this way, as St. Paul
says, he must aim to be:

*Saintly and religious, filled with faith and love, patient
and gentle.* (1 Tm 6:11)

His is a demanding life and he needs your prayers, your
encouragement and your cooperation since in the parish as
in the whole Church:

Each part must be equally concerned for all the others.
(1 Cor 12:25)

Building Parish Community

(54) Have you ever, after prayer and thought, suggested
how your own parish community could be improved?
More important, have you ever made it clear that you are
ready and willing to do something toward that end? The

first step is always a readiness to put time and effort into the needs of your parish community. Ideas alone are not enough; recipes don't bake cakes.

(55) The purpose of parish pastoral councils, so strongly recommended by Vatican II, is to give you an opportunity to become seriously involved in building your parish into a real Christian community. How can the modern parish be built into a really united community of love? Nobody knows the full answer in every detail. It will come only as a result of a continuing and united effort on the part of all who belong to the parish. All, whether priests, religious, or laity, need to learn how to listen to each other as Christians. This is the first step in Christian dialogue and in the building of Christian community. The art of listening does not come easily. It requires genuine charity. It is only when we love others that we are ready to listen to them.

(56) Dialogue requires humility, an awareness that none of us has all the answers. It must always be seen as a prayerful and holy exercise. It is the giving and receiving of truth. It requires great courage at times, because often it is easier to keep silent and not speak out than to say what we believe to be right. It always requires an attitude of prayer, an ability to pray sincerely with others.

(57) Shared spontaneous prayer is the best preparation for fruitful dialogue. The ultimate aim of dialogue is never a desire to vindicate anyone's particular idea, but rather a humble and prayerful search for the will of God. Those in authority always have the final say in discerning what is the will of God, but they may never refuse to listen prayerfully to the community.

(58) There is a growing conviction today that there is need
for much smaller groups of people to form *primary
communities* within the average large parish, particularly
big city parishes. Groups of four or five families who meet
together regularly in one another's homes for prayer, scripture reading, study and dialogue soon grow into very vital
Christian communities.

(59) Through their shared prayer and genuine charity they
learn to listen lovingly to one another's needs, to be
concerned for one another, to support and encourage one
another. They become a powerful witness of Christian love
to an unbelieving world. How beautifully like the early
Christian communities this can be. The growing custom
of small groups of Christians meeting, praying, and worshiping together can help to build up small primary communities of this kind. We have Christ's guarantee that he
will be present in a very special way in such communities
as these:

*Where two or three meet in my name, I shall be there
with them.* (Mt 18:20)

(60) He gives very special manifestations of his presence
to communities that are united in love and prayer. A
parish which has primary communities of this kind cannot
fail to show real life and vitality. The Church lives in a
special way in such a parish. The people meet and recognize Jesus in each other, especially in the poor and the
needy. Their Sunday Mass takes on new depths of meaning.
Like the Christians we read about in the Acts of the Apostles, they become deeply aware that the Mass is the center
of their Christian community life. When they offer each
other a sign of peace at Mass it becomes a very genuine

and meaningful token indeed. They have the joy and peace
of knowing that they are alive with a very life of Christ
which unites them and they are not going to God in loneliness of isolation, but

> *that the saints together* (i.e., themselves) *make a unity
> in the work of service, building up the body of Christ.*
> (Eph 4:12)

Part of God's Household

(61) The Church looks forward in "joyful hope"; the
Church is basically a celebration of victory already
won:

> *You see this city? Here God lives among men. He will
> make his home among them; they shall be his people,
> and he will be their God; his name is God-with-them.
> He will wipe away all tears from their eyes; there will
> be no more death, and no more mourning or
> sadness. . . .* (Rv 21:3-4)

(62) The Church is a witness to a risen Jesus and expresses
this often in her prayers with "Alleluia" which means
"Praise the Lord!" The Spirit of the Church is "not a spirit
of timidity but a spirit of power, of love and self-control"
(2 Tm 1:7). Nor is it a spirit of sadness or slavery:

> *Where the Spirit of the Lord is* (and surely he is in his
> Church) *there is freedom.* (2 Cor 3:17)

St. Peter tells us:

> *So behave like free men, and never use your freedom
> as an excuse for wickedness. Have respect for
> everyone and love for our community.* (1 Pt 2:16-17)

(63) But for us, the real source of joy is that we belong to
     God's family, to God's people already saved through
their faith, by the power of the Holy Spirit.

> *So you are no longer aliens or foreign visitors: you are*
> *citizens like all the saints, and part of God's household.*
> *You are part of a building that has the apostles and the*
> *prophets for its foundations, and Christ Jesus himself*
> *for its main cornerstone; and you too, in him, are being*
> *built into a house where God lives, in the Spirit.*
> (Eph 2:19-22)

(64) This is the Church — one, holy, catholic and apostolic
     — founded by Jesus Christ to which it is our privilege
to belong.

A Prayer for Community

> *Heavenly Father, we believe that you call us to-*
> *gether in your Church as one united people. Strengthen*
> *the bonds which unite us as brothers and sisters of*
> *your Son Jesus. Father, you alone can change our*
> *hearts and make us into the kind of people you want*
> *us to be. Make us ever more aware that you want us*
> *to be a real community united in prayer and listening*
> *reverently with our pastor for your will in our lives.*

> *Father, teach us how to listen in love to one another*
> *and to our pastor, and teach him how to listen to us*
> *in the way you want him to listen. Father, without*
> *you we are incapable of growing into a community of*
> *love where your Spirit dwells, but you can change our*
> *hearts; send your Spirit now to fill us and change us.*

Plant deep down in us a great love for you and a deep love and concern for one another.

Teach us how to listen when your Spirit speaks to us through others. Teach us how to discern the voice of your Spirit in the voices of others, especially in the voice of our pastor. Show us how to love one another as you want us to love.

POINTS FOR DISCUSSION

1.   "The Blessed Trinity is the basis of Christian community." Discuss.

2.   How do we show that God calls us as a people rather than as individuals?

3.   Why is it necessary for the Church's leaders to listen to the people in order to discern the voice of the Holy Spirit?

4.   How can small prayer and study groups help form a parish into a vital Christian community?

REVIEW

1. People need people to be truly human and fully happy. T F

2. Moses sealed God's friendship for man with the sprinkling of blood. T F

3. Man chose God before God chose him. T F

4. God's people succeeded because they were numerically large. T F

5. The Church — those who believe Jesus is the Lord — is God's new people. T F

6. God's people have no more power than any other group of people. T F

7. The Church like any other organization exists solely for the good of its members. T F

8. The Church is Christ alive again in the world today. T F

9. God gives different vocations and ministries to different people to show forth Christ today. T F

10. The first work of the people of God is
    to love one another.　　　　　　　　T　　F

11. A Christian must have priorities which
    he will never compromise.　　　　　　T　　F

12. Loving one another is not important if
    we worship God sincerely.　　　　　　T　　F

13. We are not full members of the
    Church unless we are actively
    concerned for one another.　　　　　　T　　F

14. The most important gift in the Church
    is authority.　　　　　　　　　　　　T　　F

15. The Church upholds the truth and
    keeps it safe.　　　　　　　　　　　　T　　F

16. The Church is being led into all truth
    gradually.　　　　　　　　　　　　　T　　F

17. The people of God is a democracy.　　T　　F

18. Every Christian shares in the guidance
    of the Church.　　　　　　　　　　　T　　F

19. The pope has all the answers in his
    own mind.　　　　　　　　　　　　　T　　F

20. The parish priest has all the gifts
    necessary for a good parish.　　　　　T　　F

21. Real concern for one another begins when
we learn to listen deeply to the other.   T   F

22. Jesus is present anywhere two or three
people come together in his name.   T   F

23. The Church is the family of God to which
we can belong by faith and baptism.   T   F

Chapter 7

A CHRISTIAN CONSCIENCE

(1)   In this chapter we look at the question which bothers many good people today — "What is right and what is wrong, or has it all changed?" It is true that many church laws are changing. This can be confusing for those of us taught to see right and wrong in terms of obedience and disobedience to laws. "But is this not so?" you may say. To answer this question, we shall have to look deeply once again at the meaning of the words which we say in the Our Father. "Thy will be done on earth as it is in heaven."

Obedience to God Is Love Made Visible

(2)   By faith we accept Jesus and all that he says; by love we recognize all that he has done for us; by keeping his commands we show our faith and love in an unmistakable way. St. Paul calls this the "obedience of faith" (Rom 1:5), and Jesus made this very clear in these words:

Anybody who receives my commandments and keeps them will be the one who loves me. (Jn 14:21)

Our obedience to Jesus is our love for him made visible.

157

On another occasion he said:

*Why do you call me "Lord, Lord" and not do what I
say? Everyone who comes to me and listens to my
words and acts on them—I will show you what he is
like. He is like a man who when he built his house dug,
and dug deep, and laid the foundations on rock; when
the river was in flood, it bore down on that house but
could not shake it. It was so well built. But the one
who listens and does nothing is like the man who built
his house on soil, with no foundations; as soon as the
river bore down on it, it collapsed; and what a ruin that
house became.* (Lk 6:46-49)

(3)   One of the first bishops of the Church, St. James,
       wrote:

*Take the case, my brothers, of someone who has never
done a single good act but claims that he has faith.
Will that faith save him? . . . If good works do not go
with it, it is quite dead . . . . Do realize, you senseless
man, that faith without good deeds is useless.*
(Jas 2:14,17,20)

(4)   This is very clear and shows us that faith which is
       genuine, and love which is authentic always result in
good works. But why should we do good works? Why is it
so important that we obey Jesus' commands? To answer
this question let us look first to Jesus himself.

Love and Obedience in Jesus

*My aim is to do not my own will, but the will of him
who sent me.* (Jn 5:30)

(5)   In these words Jesus tells us why he came on earth and the reason for every thought, word and action of his life. It was to do what his Father was asking him to do. He even called this his food:

> *My food is to do the will of him who sent me and to complete his work.* (Jn 4:34)

It was his first motive on coming into the womb of Mary.

> *God, here I am! I am coming to obey your will.*
> (Heb 10:7)

Whether he obeyed Mary, learned his trade from St. Joseph, played with other children in the street, preached by the lakeside, rested when he was tired, ate when he was hungry, or suffered on the cross, it was always in obedience to his Father's will for our salvation.

(6)   As we have seen in the last chapter, the people of God are Jesus now living again by the power of His Holy Spirit. He is again walking, working, praying, preaching, healing, suffering, dying and rising again in us. And just like his first life in Palestine, he wants to live it in obedience to his Father's will. When a Christian expresses his faith by doing the will of God, it is Jesus who does it through him. This is why he said:

> *Anyone who does the will of my Father in heaven is my brother, my sister and mother.* (Mt 12:50)

For this reason St. John could remind the first Christians:

> *Anyone who does the will of God remains for ever.*
> (1 Jn 2:17)

To the Jews who believed in him Jesus said:

If you make my word your home you will indeed be my disciples. (Jn 8:31)

(7) "Home" is a very intimate word. By using it Jesus tells us how deeply we must be committed to accepting every word he speaks and how it must therefore influence every part and every moment of our lives.

Dedication to God's Will in Us

Hold perfectly and securely to the will of God. (Col 4:12)

(8) This was the intention in a prayer of one of the first Christians, Epaphras, for his fellow Christians at Colossae. It should be our frequent prayer for one another too. Nothing else in life matters as much as this. Without this nothing in life matters at all. Parents should often pray for this for their children and for each other.

Paul in his letter to the same people wrote:

We have never failed to pray for you, and what we ask God is that through perfect wisdom and spiritual understanding you should reach the fullest knowledge of his will. So you will be able to lead the kind of life God expects of you, a life acceptable to him in all its aspects; showing the results in all the good actions you do . . . . (Col 1:9-10)

(9) This is Paul's wish, that Jesus keep on living in his Church and keep on obeying his Father's will in the life of each Christian. We live out our new life in Christ

when we are permitting him to love his Father through our lived-out obedience to his commands.

God's Will and God's Presence

He who sent me is with me, and he has not left me to myself, for I always do what pleases him. (Jn 8:29)

(10) Just as the Father lived in Jesus because Jesus always did what pleased him, so we too can be sure of God's presence in our lives when we are willing to do what pleases him.

But, on the other hand, when a member of the Church refuses to do the will of the Father, he must remind himself that when Peter suggested Jesus should not go through his suffering and death, Jesus said to him:

Get behind me, Satan! You are an obstacle in my path, because the way you think is not God's way but man's. (Mt 16:23)

(11) We could be an obstacle in the way of Jesus' living for his Father in his Church by refusing to obey what we know to be the will of God. But this obedience must begin in our hearts, it must be deep obedience.

Deep Obedience

If your virtue goes no deeper than that of the scribes and Pharisees, you will never get into the kingdom of heaven. (Mt 5:20)

(12) Most of the scribes and Pharisees were quite strict

about observing the law; in fact they were "experts" at it. Why then did Jesus condemn them? Because they kept only the letter of the law and their hearts were not open to God. Doing what God wants is important but our hearts must be humble before God first. If our hearts are not right, it does not matter how well we behave; unless there is real love for our Lord and for our neighbor in our hearts, then we too must accept what Jesus said to the scribes and Pharisees:

> *Alas for you, scribes and Pharisees, you hypocrites! You who are like whitewashed tombs that look handsome on the outside, but inside are full of dead men's bones and every kind of corruption.* (Mt 23:27)

(13) Jesus gave us many examples of what he meant. Here is one of them:

> *You have learnt how it was said: you must not commit adultery. But I say this to you: if a man looks at a woman lustfully, he has already committed adultery with her in his heart.* (Mt 5:27-28)

Others can see our behavior, but let us hear God.

> *It is I who search hearts and loins and give to each of you what your behavior deserves.* (Rv 2:23)

(14) It was because Jesus could see their simple, repentant hearts that he was more pleased with the prostitutes than with the priests, with sinners rather than with those who posed as the saints of those days. Let us look at Jesus, at his Sacred Heart.

The Hearts of Jesus and Mary

The world must be brought to know that I love the Father . . . . (Jn 14:31)

(15) After speaking these words which tell us about how his heart was before his heavenly Father, Jesus left the Last Supper room to begin his suffering in the garden of Gethsemani. In these words he tells us that the source of his behavior, the reason for his action, was his love for his Father. This is how it must be with all of us. We must live for the Father because we recognize his love for us and love him in return. No matter how moral our behavior is, without this it is not Christian behavior.

(16) Mary had the perfect posture of heart before God: "I am the handmaid of the Lord," and so she was willing to let God's will be done for her. "Let what you have said be done to me." Here she is the model of the whole Church and every member of the Church. In these words, because of her open and available heart, God used her and she became the mother of the Church, whose first member she was through her having been conceived without sin.

(17) God can do and still does "great things" with those of us who completely open our hearts, like Mary did, to his will. He will use our hands; our hands will become actively the hands of Jesus in the world if our hearts are like the heart of Mary before his will. Jesus stressed the importance of the heart for Christian morality very often.

Worship Implies Obedience

These people honor me with lip service, while their hearts are far from me. (Mt 15:8)

(18) The religious men of his day went to church and
        prayed as we do, but to some of them he addressed
those words and then he continued:

The worship they offer me is worthless. (Mt 15:9)

(19) This could be true of you and me, if our hearts are not
        close to the Sacred Heart of Jesus in love and rever-
ence, listening to his will.

From the heart come evil intentions: murder, adultery,
fornication, theft, perjury, slander. These are the
things that make a man unclean. (Mt 15:19)

(20) To his people St. James wrote about the importance
        of the heart too:

But if at heart you have the bitterness of jealousy or
self-seeking ambition, never make any claims for
yourself or cover up the truth with lies. (Jas 3:14)

(21) The truth is always what is in our hearts, not what
        appears on the surface. If our hearts are right we have
taken the first and fundamental step in Christian morality
because:

A good man draws what is good from the store of
goodness in his heart; a bad man draws what is bad
from the store of badness. For man's words flow out of
what fills his heart. (Lk 6:45)

(22) It is important to remember that good actions or bad
        actions come from our hearts, from the center of our
personalities, from our core freedom. The words we use or
the actions we perform are just signs of the attitude of our
hearts before God.

How Do We Know the Will of God?

(23) But how do I know what is God's will at any moment? How am I to know the best way to act in a given situation? How can I know what is right and what is wrong? How am I to know what I ought to do or to avoid here and now? The answer can be stated very simply — I must follow my conscience.

(24) There are no exceptions to this if it is properly understood. I must always follow my conscience.

I do my best to keep a clear conscience at all times before God and men. (Acts 24:16)

(25) In all my activity I am bound to follow my conscience faithfully, in order that I may come to God for whom I was created. I must follow my conscience not only in particular cases, but in every case. Conscience must always be my ultimate guide. To follow it faithfully is permanently my duty.

(26) The reason for this is that to follow one's conscience is equal to carrying out God's will in one's life. Conscience is a God-given light which must guide us on our path through life. When God gives us his will through our conscience he does not suggest; he decrees. Obedience to conscience is direct obedience to God. Once you are prepared to follow your conscience you have but one purpose; this is to carry out God's will. With total and unconditional abandonment to God's loving care you decide to do whatever he asks of you at any time.

(27) This means living constantly in God's presence. It means that the attitude of your heart is prayerful searching for and a radar-like sensitivity to God's will, combined with a readiness to carry it out when it is discovered. When you follow your conscience you always do what is pleasing to God. A "clear conscience" about which St. Paul speaks in the quotation above is the voice of God speaking to me at every moment of my life. In the final analysis, we find what God wants of us through our conscience.

What Is My Conscience?

(28) Conscience is not something separate from me. Conscience is *myself judging about whether a certain action is right or wrong.* Conscience is the most secret core and sanctuary of my person. There I am alone with God whose voice echoes in my heart.

(29) By my conscience, I mean my awareness of myself as a free and responsible person who can choose between different ways of thinking and acting. If I think of myself as free, I must think of myself as responsible for the way I use this freedom. I use this freedom to choose between different values.

(30) My conscience tells me that by my free choice I can change something in the lives of others — for instance, take your pen from you, or give you money when you need it. My conscience also tells me that by my free choice I can change myself. For instance I can take a trip, get married, work harder or become a more generous person.

(31) Looked at from this point of view, my conscience is

my awareness that it is *I* who must decide to make myself the kind of person I am going to be. It is *I* finally who must decide how I am going to respond to God's love and whether I am going to be with him in heaven or not. But, of course, my conscience must be functioning well, it must be clear.

Conscience Must Be Clear and Sincere

A pure heart, a clear conscience and a sincere faith.
(1 Tm 1:5)

(32) We cannot take for granted that our conscience is based on this "pure heart" and "sincere faith" which St. Paul speaks to Timothy about.

(33) Or, very simply, we cannot automatically be sure that we have a "clear conscience." But if we are going to follow it and if it is to be the faithful echo of God's will, it is surely important that it be pure, sincere and clear. We have a serious obligation to make sure that this is so, rather like the obligation a pilot has to ensure that his radar equipment is always in good working order. He must be sure that it is picking up the right signals and doing this accurately. Each of us must make sure that our conscience is in good working order. In other words, my conscience must be *formed* as well as *followed*.

(34) My conscience is not a computer programmed with answers for every situation; no, it is *all of me* equipped to search for the right answers in every situation. There is no slot-machine morality. I will never have a complete set of ready-made answers, because situations in my life are

always changing. I must always keep my conscience informed, alive and delicately attuned to judge in each situation as it comes along. Thus forming my conscience goes
on all through my life.

In every new situation, if my conscience is going to
relay to me the will of God accurately, I need to consider
four steps:

(35) (a) *Find the facts clearly:*
I must try to understand all the aspects of the situation
about which I must judge. I cannot make a decision unless
I have done my best to find the data, such as what the
Church teaches about this, what are the pressures on myself here and now, and what are the rights of others in this
situation?

(36) (b) *Weigh the facts sincerely:*
The same facts in different situations have different
value, so I must decide how important the facts are in this
situation, and even which of the facts is the more important
here. St. Paul calls this our "inner mental dialogue"
(Rom 2:15).

(37) (c) *Judge the facts fairly:*
Here I come to the heart of conscience. After I have
weighed the facts I judge that I ought or ought not to do this
action. I must try to form this judgment without any bias.

(38) (d) *Act on the facts wisely:*
Then I must be willing to follow the judgment which I
have made, namely, to carry out or not to carry out that
action which I judged to be right or wrong.

(39) This decision or willingness to do what I judge I ought to do is not automatic. I could make the right judgment but then fail to carry it out. It depends on the posture of my heart, whether it is more *for* God or more *away from* him, and whether I usually act the way he wants or usually the other way. Every time I decide to do what I know God wants I am more likely to do so the next time. Every time I refuse to do it, I am also less likely to do so the next time.

Pressures on Conscience

(40) To judge the facts and to weigh them honestly, to make an unbiased judgment, and then do the right thing is to live by the will of God. But this is not easy at any step. Since we ourselves are involved in the judging and deciding, and since we have a tendency to be selfish, there is a likelihood that because a decision is going to cost me something, I make it in a way that it will not cost me anything. It is so easy to mistake self-interest for the voice of God. Though we are full of good intentions, we are inclined to find excuses for what we like to do or to avoid doing. This is the result of original sin. Even St. Paul felt it and said so in this way:

> *I cannot understand my own behavior. I fail to carry out the things I want to do, and I find myself doing the very things I hate . . . . I carry out the sinful things I do not want . . . .* (Rom 7:15,19)

(41) Our conscience then is weakened by original sin and maybe by many personal sins. Consequently, it is no longer a pure and undamaged sounding board of God's voice within us. It will certainly be able to tell us that we must do God's will always, but it does not always tell us

clearly enough what God's will is in a particular case. God speaks through our conscience but we are inclined to be selective in what we hear. The voice of our own selfishness is inclined to blur the delicate voice of God speaking to us. Usually we will need help to hear the voice of God in the voice of our conscience.

(42) So, if I am sincere in my faith and in my search for God's will in my conscience, I will try to allow for the effect of blind spots and biases in myself. If I am sincere I will have a certain humility and hesitance in my search for the will of God.

(43) I will usually stop short of absolute assurance in my judgments and I will try to keep open to future development and further refinement or even to a revision of my present position. I surely recognize that if I am to be able to find and express what is good, I must be truly good myself. And most of us should be very slow to judge that we are permanently good in this sense. So, we recognize that in forming our conscience we need help from the presence of the Holy Spirit in others, i.e., in the community.

Truth and Love Are Always God's Will
(44) As we have seen in an earlier chapter, the church-community is Jesus living again. He is alive and speaking still in every true, noble, good, pure, lovable, honorable, virtuous and praiseworthy thing which appears in the world. That is why St. Paul told the Ephesians:

> *If we live by truth and in love, we shall grow up in all ways into Christ, who is the head by whom the whole body is fitted and joined together.* (Eph 4:15-16)

If we are ready to do this, our conscience will be very open to the voice of God's Holy Spirit.

(45) The Church has preserved the word of God for us in the scriptures. In them we are told that the main characteristic of Christian behavior is self-giving and self-forgetful love modeled on the love of Jesus:

> *This is my commandment: Love one another as I have loved you.* (Jn 15:12)

(46) The norm of action for the Christian is not reasonableness but the demands of love. The Christian is concerned with God's goodness and not with his own welfare. Because he is allowing Jesus to relive his life in him, he is filled with love of the Father and of his fellowmen. Morality for the Christian then becomes, as Jesus said when he was asked by the lawyer: "What must I do to inherit eternal life?"

> *You must love the Lord your God with all your heart, with all your soul, with all your strength, and with all your mind and your neighbor as yourself.* (Lk 10:27)

(47) This love which is the Holy Spirit in the heart of the Christian has both an enriching and a simplifying influence on behavior. If you really love somebody, you don't have to be constantly referring to laws and rules. Usually genuine love will ensure good behavior and good relationships. It is not that love is always a perfect protection against error of judgment or lack of generosity in doing the right thing. Even with great love one can make mistakes, but they will be recognized and repented of easily.

(48) It is true to say that if the love of God is the dominant influence in your life, you need not be overly concerned about the details of conduct. As you grow in the love of God through prayer, you will gradually get more sensitive to and more willing to do what he wants. But you will always need the help of the Christian community in forming your conscience.

God Speaks to Us Through His Church

Teach them to observe all the commands I gave you.
(Mt 28:20)

(49) Jesus spoke these words to his apostles just before he ascended into heaven. He said he had all the authority in heaven and on earth. And with this same authority he sent the leaders of his Church to teach the world all the commands he himself had given. And to his disciples when he had sent them out earlier he had said:

Anyone who listens to you listens to me. (Lk 10:16)

(50) By speaking to us in that way through his Church, Jesus helps our weakened conscience. The voice of God in our conscience can easily be drowned out by self-love, self-interest or human pride. Since the fall of our first parents, man needs further help to discern clearly the voice of God amidst the turmoil of his own passions. Jesus founded his Church and gave her his own authority to help us discover his divine will through a well-developed conscience.

(51) Some may think that there is opposition here. But the authority of the Church has not been given as an op-

ponent of personal conscience. It has been given as a help and a guide to conscience. A well-developed conscience will recognize its own weakness and its need for assistance. To deny the need for the guidance of the Church is to deny that one is sinful.

(52) A well-developed conscience has an ever-growing respect for the voice of the Church because it discerns therein the voice of God. It is possible that in an individual case a person, after prolonged thought and prayer, feels he must act at variance with church teaching. There is nothing sinful about this provided that he is open to further searching and further enlightenment in his continuing efforts to find the will of God.

Our Conscience Will Judge Us

We shall all have to stand before the judgment seat of God. (Rom 14:10)

(53) We shall be judged ultimately according to the degree of fidelity with which we have followed our personal conscience.

In every moral decision there is a point where we stand alone before God. No one — neither husband nor wife, neither father nor mother, neither priest nor pope — can take responsibility for our decision. We may never obey another against our own conscience. Nor may we ever follow our desires rather than our conscience. Our eternal destiny will depend on fidelity to our conscience.

When We Fail

(54) It is always wrong to go against one's conscience.

Everyone who knows what is the right thing to do and doesn't do it commits a sin. (Jas 4:17)

But let us not be discouraged since Jesus told us to pray for the forgiveness of our trespasses just as we pray for our daily bread.

(55) By prayer and penance God forgives us our sins because:

If anyone should sin we have our advocate with the Father, Jesus Christ, who is just; he is the sacrifice that takes our sins away. (1 Jn 2:1)

(56) There is a particular kind of sin which is very serious.

In the life of a sincere Christian it is very rare. It is a fully deliberate reversal of one's friendship for God in a serious matter.

This reversal comes from a person's deepest freedom. God compared it to the complete rejection of one's partner in marriage. It is a rejection which says the friendship is over. It is a complete turning away from the loved one. This is a *mortal sin.*

(57) If your whole heart is not in the action or if you did not honestly regard it as serious at the time, then it is not mortal sin. If there was some forgetfulness, or if you were too tired or upset to think clearly, it could not be mortal sin. If without realizing it you just got carried away, it is unlikely to have been mortal sin either.

(58) To sum up, if you are living a good Christian life of prayer, and trying generally to do the right thing as you see it, the likelihood of you committing mortal sin is very small. How could you, having loved God with fidelity, suddenly turn completely the other way?

(59) Before mortal sin can come, there will always be a *gradual deterioration* in one's friendship for God. Before total infidelity there is always gradual infidelity in any relationship. Mortal sin is the complete *no* to God with full consent and in a serious matter. Anything less should not deter one from approaching the Eucharist after the usual sincere confession of sinfulness made together before Mass.

(60) The reason why this confession is made together is because all sin offends the *community* as well as God. We must be reconciled to the community before we worship God together as his people.

Conscience and the Holy Spirit

(61) Christian morality is different from every other morality because it is more than an effort to live up to principles and laws however good. By baptism and a good conscience the Christian is in permanent contact with the person and power of the Holy Spirit, who guides the Church and every member of it. This makes no sense to those who lack faith.

> *An unspiritual person is one who does not accept anything of the Spirit of God; he sees it all as nonsense; it is beyond his understanding because it can only be understood by means of the Spirit.* (1 Cor 2:14)

(62) We must be "people of the Spirit" (1 Cor 3:1-4)• by
      faith in Jesus if our conscience is to be our guide to the
voice of God within us. The Holy Spirit speaks to the heart
which lives by faith. Unless we are living "under the influence of the Holy Spirit" (1 Cor 12:3) there is a danger that
the voice we hear will not be God's. St. Paul stressed that
his conscience never acted in isolation:

> *I say it in union with Christ, it is the truth, my conscience*
> *in union with the Holy Spirit assures me of it too.*
> (Rom 9:1)

(63) If we live a life of faith expressed in prayer our moral
      behavior will be an expression of our love of God.
Finding his will can never then be difficult.

(64) St. Paul stressed the link between the Holy Spirit and
      Christian morality in his letter to the people of Galatia:

> *Let me put it like this; if you are guided by the Spirit*
> *you will be in no danger of yielding to self-indulgence,*
> *since self-indulgence is the opposite of the Spirit, the*
> *Spirit is totally against such a thing. . . . When self-*
> *indulgence is at work the results are obvious,*
> *fornication, gross indecency and sexual irresponsibility,*
> *idolatry and sorcery; feuds and wrangling, jealousy,*
> *bad temper and quarrels: disagreements, factions,*
> *envy, drunkenness, orgies and similar things. I warn*
> *you now, as I warned you before: those who behave*
> *like this will not inherit the kingdom of God. What the*
> *Spirit brings is very different: love, joy, peace, patience,*
> *kindness, goodness, trustfulness, gentleness and self-*
> *control.* (Gal 5:16-22)

Since the Spirit is our life, let us be directed by the Spirit. (Gal 5:25)

(65) The Spirit brings man to a new awareness of God's love for him; the Spirit makes man aware of his divine sonship and of his fellowmen and of the love that therefore must obtain among all men.

(66) Urged by the love which the Spirit pours into our hearts, the spiritual man turns away from the pull of sin and self and is drawn only by the love of the Father.

(67) So, the Spirit represents freedom from law, for whatever restrictions the law could put on him, whatever good it asks him to do, all this the true Christian already wants to do and much more. And so the life of the Spirit represents freedom from sin also because of the power it gives to resist temptation. The Holy Spirit is thus the source of true Christian morality.

We Have the Strength of His Power

Grow strong in the Lord with the strength of his power. (Eph 6:10)

(68) God's law is not a cold command given without deep concern. It is not a promise made without power to achieve its reward. Our heavenly Father gives us the very power of Jesus through his Spirit as we pray, receive the sacraments and live by faith. We have God's armor, and we can rely on that. Here is how he tells us through St. Paul:

Finally, grow strong in the Lord, with the strength of his

*power. Put God's armor on so as to be able to resist
the devil's tactics. For it is not against human enemies
that we have to struggle, but against sovereignties and
the powers who originate the darkness in this world,
the spiritual army of evil in the heavens. That is why
you must rely on God's armor, or you will not be able
to put up any resistance when the worst happens, or
have enough resources to hold your ground.*
(Eph 6:10-13)

In another place in the same letter St. Paul says:

*We are God's work of art, created in Christ to live the
good life as from the beginning he had meant us to
live it.* (Eph 2:10)

The Example of Mary

(69) Mary's life was not spectacular. She had the great
privilege of being the mother of God, but when another woman said that she was blessed on account of this,
Jesus said:

*Still happier those who hear the word of God and keep
it.* (Lk 11:28)

(70) This was the story of her life in fulfillment of the
moment when she spoke her autobiography so simply:

*I am the handmaid of the Lord, let what you have
said be done to me.* (Lk 1:38)

With this posture of heart, we will always hear the word
of God and keep it.

Psalm 119 is a beautiful prayer in praise of the law of

God. Some selected verses from it will help us. Say them prayerfully now.

A Prayer:

Ah, how happy those of blameless life
who walk in the law of Yahweh!
How happy those who respect his decrees
and seek him with their whole heart . . .

If I can concentrate on your every commandment
I can never be put to shame.
I thank you for an upright heart
schooled in your rules of righteousness . . .

I have treasured your promises in my heart,
since I have no wish to sin against you.
How blessed are you, Yahweh!
Teach me your statutes . . .

I run the way of your commandments
since you have set me free.
Expound to me the way of your statutes, Yahweh,
and I will always respect them.

Explain to me how to respect your law
and how to observe it wholeheartedly.
Guide me in the path of your commandments
since my delight is there . . .

Let me observe your law unfailingly
forever and ever.
So, having sought your precepts,
I shall walk in all freedom.

POINTS FOR DISCUSSION

1. How can a Christian's obedience to God's law be a continuation of Jesus' obedience to his Father's will?

2. Why is it necessary to know the Church's teaching before I can have an informed conscience?

3. List the four practical steps which are necessary in order to make moral decisions in accordance with the will of God.

4. Why do we all need help in forming our consciences?

R E V I E W

1. True faith leads to obedience to God's word.   T   F

2. Jesus showed his love for his Father by his obedience.   T   F

3. In his body the Church, Jesus wants to continue to obey his Father.   T   F

4. Simply doing the letter of the law is Christian obedience.   T   F

5. Serious sin can be committed in the heart.   T   F

6. A Christian should show his love of the Father by his life as Jesus did.   T   F

7. Mass going can be useless unless we generally try to obey God's word.   T   F

8. Obedience of the heart is the first and most necessary obedience.   T   F

9. My conscience is the source of knowing God's will in my life.   T   F

10. A Christian must always follow his conscience.   T   F

11. Unless I live continually in God's presence, my conscience will be unclear.   T   F

12. Conscience is a special and separate
    part of the Christian person.   T   F

13. By my conscience I am now making myself
    the person I shall one day become.   T   F

14. A Christian conscience is programmed
    with all the right answers.   T   F

15. Conscience formation goes on all
    through one's life.   T   F

16. It is easy to weigh the facts sincerely.   T   F

17. We automatically do what we know
    is right.   T   F

18. Original sin has left us with a need of
    help in forming our consciences.   T   F

19. Conscience is usually a pure sounding
    board of God's voice.   T   F

20. Truth and life are always God's will.   T   F

21. A well-developed conscience listens to
    the teaching Church.   T   F

22. It is possible to act at variance with
    church teaching in good conscience.   T   F

23. The Christian conscience must always
    be guided by the Holy Spirit.   T   F

Chapter 8

OUR CHRISTIAN WITNESS

(1)   In Jesus God the Father reaches down to us in love and gives us the power to reach up to him in response to his love. This is the *good news* — the Christian gospel. He offers it to *all men*.

(2)   His Son Jesus was the evidence of this; he witnessed to this. By his coming he announced the good news of salvation to all men. He made God's name known. In the scriptures, a person's name represents the person. So Jesus came to make God known and to offer God's personal friendship to all men. Speaking in prayer to his heavenly Father at the end of his earthly life, he said:

*I have made your name known to them
and will continue to make it known.* (Jn 17:26)

(3)   Notice that although he is about to die and to leave the world in his human existence, he states that he will *continue* to make the Father's name, i.e., his person, known. How does he continue to do this? How did he hope to keep his promise to do it? He does it through us, his Church, in which and through which he lives again. It is our privilege to permit Jesus to continue making God's name known to

men through us. He needs us; he depends on us to save the world.

The Witness and Work of Jesus

(4)   At a most solemn moment in his life — during his Last Supper with his apostles — Jesus said:

Eternal life is this:
to know you, the only true God
and Jesus Christ whom you have sent. (Jn 17:3)

Jesus' whole life— his prayer, his years as a carpenter, his preaching, his miracles, his death and resurrection — had only one purpose, to give men this eternal life for the glory of his Father:

I have come so that they may have life and have it to
the full. (Jn 10:10)

This is the life which we received through faith and baptism into the people of God.

The Witness and Work of the Holy Spirit

(5)   We studied the work of the Holy Spirit in an earlier chapter. It is to continue the work of Jesus in us, to witness to him and to glorify him:

When the Advocate comes, whom I shall send you from
the Father, the Spirit of truth who issues from the
Father he will be my witness. (Jn 15:26)

It is through him that the work of Jesus will be brought to perfection. It is through him that we receive the commission and the power to witness to Jesus.

Our Work of Witness

(6)   At the same time that Jesus told his followers that the
Holy Spirit would witness to him, he continued:

And you too will be my witnesses. (Jn 15:27)

It is our duty and our happy privilege to glorify Jesus by
continuing to proclaim his message and pass on his power
to the world. In the same chapter of St. John's Gospel, we
hear Jesus saying to his followers:

If they kept my word, they will keep yours as well.
(Jn 15:20)

(7)   He wants his word to continue to be heard through us.
Our voice can be his; it must be if we are living in the
faith. He identifies with us in everything, telling us that
men will react to us as they did to him:

If they persecuted me, they will persecute you too.
(Jn 15:20)

This witness began when he assured his Church:

*You will be my witnesses not only in Jerusalem but
throughout Judea and Samaria, and indeed to the ends
of the earth.* (Acts 1:8)

(8)   The apostles to whom he spoke these words did not in
fact see the "ends of the earth" but they represented
the Church which has since then been proclaiming the word
of God everywhere. Jesus foresaw this and prayed about
it at his Last Supper:

*I pray not only for these, but for those also who through
their words will believe in me.* (Jn 17:20)

We are those people.

Witness to What?

(9) Just as Jesus had foretold, his followers were persecuted even shortly after his ascension into heaven.
They were arrested and imprisoned but they were rescued
by one of God's angels who said as he led them out:

> Go and stand in the Temple, and tell the people all
> about this new Life. (Acts 5:20)

Of course they did this but were arrested again and brought
to stand before the full senate of Israel, the Sanhedrin.
Once again they were told to stop preaching, but Peter gave
a brief summary of what he planned to do and why. In this
summary we have a precious statement of what every Christian is called on to witness to the world:

> Obedience to God comes before obedience to men; it
> was the God of our ancestors who raised up Jesus,
> but it was you who had him executed by hanging on a
> tree. By his own right hand God has now raised him up
> to be leader and savior to give repentance and
> forgiveness of sins through him to Israel. We are
> witnesses to all this, we and the Holy Spirit.
> (Acts 5:29-32)

(10) The apostles risked their lives just to say this. We
know that eventually many of them were actually killed
for their witness to this faith. Because it was the mission
given them by Jesus, nothing — even the loss of their lives
— would prevent them from passing on the good news so
that others would share their joy in it. After the worship of
God, this witness or *telling others of Jesus* is the purpose for
which the Church exists.

(11) So our witness is to Jesus and our message is about him. It is not primarily about certain truths or about the Church. We aim to convert men to Jesus as he lives in the Church by his risen life. They must each meet Jesus by faith in a very personal way and submit themselves entirely to him. They must be converted in the way conversion was described in the second chapter of this book.

(12) There is a danger that we teach people Christian moral behavior or Christian social principles before we help them meet the source of these — Jesus. There is a danger that we have them accept Christian doctrines before they accept Christ. There is even a danger that men will receive God's sacraments without faith. The aim of our Christian witness, whether it be by our lives, by our words or by our prayers, is that others will first of all repent, then accept Jesus as their personal savior and receive the Holy Spirit. This is done in and through the Church. But we must not present the Church to people as a system or an organization to which they merely submit. We must present it as the body of the risen Christ.

The Church Has a Mission to Witness

(13) The people of God can never be a settled and self-satisfied community. It must always be reaching out to invite others to hear the good news that Jesus is the Lord, that God loves man and that he desires the salvation of all men. To think that the Church is passive and that it does not reach out in order to draw others into its community and into a share in its life, would be to deny its very nature. If it ever did this, it would cease to be the Church of Jesus Christ. This is because his final words were a command to

witness, a command to offer membership in God's family
to all men:

> *Go, therefore, make disciples of all nations; baptize*
> *them in the name of the Father and of the Son and of*
> *the Holy Spirit, and teach them to observe all the com-*
> *mands I gave you. . . .* (Mt 28:19-20)

We Have a Mission to Witness

(14) We are God's people and so it is we who have this
mission together. It is to us that Jesus said, "Go, make
disciples." Our privilege is to be his missionaries, or mes-
sengers of his love to mankind. St. Paul says:

> *People must think of us as Christ's servants, stewards*
> *entrusted with the mysteries of God. What is expected*
> *of stewards is that each one should be found worthy*
> *of his trust.* (1 Cor 4:1-2)

Do we really know this? Do we realize the privilege and
obligation which are ours? We are stewards of God's mysteries. Are we faithful in doing what a good steward does
— passing on the word of God to others? We must answer
that question honestly in our hearts between ourselves and
God.

(15) It may help to compare ourselves with two other Christians — Peter and John — who after imprisonment
and a warning simply said:

> *We cannot stop proclaiming what we have seen and*
> *heard.* (Acts 4:20)

This was because they remembered what Jesus had said:

You did not choose me
no, I chose you;
and I commissioned you
to go out and to bear fruit,
fruit that will last. (Jn 15:16)

This is as true of you and me as it was of them; we are chosen and we are commissioned to spread the truth of God's love to others.

We Have a Word to Say

(16) God spoke his word to the world in Jesus:

The Word was made flesh and lived among us.
(Jn 1:14)

This Jesus lives in you and me through faith and baptism. He wishes to keep on speaking God's word of love and salvation to the world through us. In the supper room, just before his death, we hear Jesus pray to his heavenly Father:

I pray not only for these but for those also who through
their words will believe in me. (Jn 17:20)

Through your words, many can believe in him; this is your privilege. Your silence can be an enforced silence on Jesus who wishes to witness his Father's love to others through you.

We Have Invitations to Offer

(17) It is true that the first stage of salvation has already taken place by the death and resurrection of Jesus; salvation is available to all men. But unless they know this, they cannot accept or refuse it.

But they will not ask for his help unless they believe
in him, and they will not believe in him unless they have
heard of him, and they will not hear of him unless they
get a preacher. (Rom 10:14)

It is not that we are all called to preach in the usual sense
of the word; but we are all called to speak, to tell our
friends about God's saving grace if they have not already
accepted it. God has given us their invitation to eternal
happiness and we should offer it to them in some way.
Later in this chapter we shall see how.

We Have the Power to Witness

(18) To witness to Jesus, to tell others that he is God's love
        made visible and that they can experience this love in
their lives calls for some courage. Before the coming of
the Holy Spirit, even St. Peter failed to do this when con-
fronted by a girl in Herod's courtyard. After he received
the Holy Spirit it was different; he had power just as Jesus
had foretold:

You will receive power when the Holy Spirit comes on
you, and then you will be my witnesses. (Act 1:8)

This is what we received at our confirmation — the same
Holy Spirit. But if we feel that we lack his power, it is because we have never made an adult act of faith in his presence within us. We will feel this power in our lives if at
some time, as adults, we reaccept the grace of our confirmation and ask with faith for the *experience* of this power
within us.

We Are the Salt of the Earth

(19) Salt gives new taste, a kind of new life, to food. Its

saltiness makes food somehow come alive. In telling us that we are not to be merely passive onlookers, but that we are to influence the world, Jesus said:

You are the salt of the earth. (Mt 5:13)

Is this true of us with the people among whom we live? Are we helping them to come alive as Christians?

We Are the Light of the World

(20) The word "light" is self-explanatory. So are the words of Jesus to us his followers when he said:

You are the light of the world. . . . No one lights a lamp to put it under a tub; they put it on a lamp-stand where it shines for everyone in the house. In the same way, your light must shine in the sight of men, so that seeing your good works, they may give praise to your Father in heaven. (Mt 5:13-16)

As Christians we need to ask ourselves if this is so in our case. Do others "see our good works" in the ordinary everyday things of life? This is the witness to which we are called.

We Are Clothed With Power

(21) It would seem senseless to push a car along the road or to go looking for gasoline if your tank is full. It seems even more senseless to feel you can't help others who are short of gas if you own an oil well yourself. Similarly, when you are hesitant about witnessing to Jesus, remember that you have the very power of Jesus within you to do it. You have only to turn on that power by faith and prayer. He said that every member of his new body, the Church, would be "clothed with power from on high" (Lk 24:49). We are members of that body. We have that power within us.

(22) This power is ours if we have truly been converted, really repented and received the Holy Spirit. We have only to live this exciting new life of intimate friendship with him to bear fruit for God.

> *I am the vine,*
> *you are the branches.*
> *Whoever remains in me with me in him,*
> *bears fruit in plenty;*
> *for cut off from me you can do nothing.* (Jn 15:5)

As Christians then we have the power to "bear fruit in plenty." Do we use this power? Or are we sitting on an oil well while the world needs fuel? Could we be whispering or silent about God's word while we have a transmitter with which to broadcast it to many others?

Witness by Loving

(23) Jesus told us that the best way to lead others to believe is by letting them see Christians show love for one another. When others see our "oneness" they will feel attracted to us. The world today appears to be grasping for this experience of community, perhaps more than ever before in history. Jesus said community would be our greatest *sign* of his presence in his people.

> *By this love you have for one another,*
> *everyone will know that you are my disciples.*
> (Jn 13:35)

It was for this he prayed to his Father:

> *Father, may they be one in us,*
> *as you are in me and I am in you,*
> *so that the world may believe it was you who sent me.*
> (Jn 17:21)

(24) Despite modern means of communication, people and peoples appear to be getting more and more alienated from one another. What an opportunity it is for us as God's people to show the world that people of different ages, backgrounds and nationalities can respect and love one another by unity on essentials and by agreeing to disagree on non-essentials. Surely we must then pray for this with St. Paul:

And may he who helps us when we refuse to give up,
help us all to be tolerant with each other,
following the example of Christ Jesus,
so that united in mind and voice
you may give glory to the God and Father of our
Lord Jesus Christ. (Rom 15:5-6)

(25) This applies in a special way to other Christian churches. Their members belong to Christ's body, through their baptism, their life of faith and their confession of Jesus as the Lord. Surely we can love them sincerely as our brothers and sisters in Christ while we wait patiently and prayerfully for complete unity with them.

It also applies to those who do not believe. We have no hope of changing people until we love them first. A simple courtesy, a gentle kindness, a small act of generosity or a genuine forgiveness by a Christian could be the first step in an unbeliever's discovery that God loves him.

(26) A good measure of our love is full-hearted acceptance of others who have different views. This is especially true in the Church today where so many different views are being held about many things. The speed of change, and the continually increasing flow of information will give rise to a still greater variety of opinions within the Church. In

the past we had little of that. Agreement is absolutely necessary only on the essentials of our faith; not on accidentals such as how we dress in Church, what hymns different groups like to use, what musical instruments younger or older people prefer, how often we say our rosary, and such like.

(27) Differences of opinion about how Christians should behave are not new. The early Christians had the same problem about fasting laws and about the strength of one another's faith. If you find it hard to hear the views of others and to accept the behavior of others in the Church today, then this may help:

> *If a person's faith is not strong enough, welcome him all the same without starting an argument . . . meat eaters must not despise the scrupulous. On the other hand, the scrupulous must not condemn those who feel free to eat anything they choose, since God has welcomed them. . . . If one man keeps certain days as holier than others, and another considers all days to be equally holy, each must be left free to hold his own opinion. . . . That is also why you should never pass judgment on a brother or treat him with contempt.*
> (Rom 14:1-10)

He sums up by saying:

> *Do all you can to live at peace with everyone.*
> (Rom 12:17)

A couple of chapters later he says:

> *It can only be to God's glory, then, for you to treat each other in the same friendly way as Christ treated you.*
> (Rom 15:7)

(28) It is up to each of us to examine his or her conscience

on this matter of genuine respect for others, especially for those who see things differently and who favor more or less change than we do. We have an obligation to find out just what is essential to our faith and what may change. Am I in danger of damaging the faith of others by appearing to attack essentials? On the other hand, am I impeding the progress of others by forcing them to hold on to what is not essential, just because it is helpful to me? We must have a profound respect and love for one another no matter what views the other holds on any subject. This is the love by which the world will know that we are truly Christian.

(29) When Jesus was invited to a wedding party on account of his mother, she showed this sensitive concern to save another's embarrassment by observing that they had no more wine. She did not have to see to this and she did not have to ask her son for a miracle, but she did. As a result we read:

He let his glory be seen and his disciples believed in him. (Jn 2:11)

Mary is our model here in giving Jesus to others by first giving ourselves in kindness, courtesy and a desire to help them. Faith is usually transmitted in a spirit of friendship or not at all.

Witness by Worship

(30) As we go out from our homes to join the parish community at Mass each week, we are witnessing to those around us. We read how the people of God grew in number right from the beginning:

They praised God and were looked up to by everyone.

Day by day the Lord added to their community those destined to be saved. (Acts 2:47)

Our regular public worship is a good example and Christian witness to those who know us.

(31) It often happens that by hearing the family next door say their family prayers together others have been led to ask questions and to believe. It has happened often too that by inviting a friend to come into the church while one makes a visit to the Blessed Sacrament, the first question is asked — a question which may lead to faith, and membership in the Church. Do we pray, or are we ashamed to be seen doing so, in a cafeteria or restaurant before we eat? Worship of God that is simple and sincere is a powerful means of leading others to God for the first time, or of bringing others back to God if they have strayed.

To pray aloud with another or for another is probably the most powerful witness of all. The next time someone asks you to pray for him or her try saying some short spontaneous prayer immediately. It is a powerful witness to the sincerity of your faith.

Witness by Christian Behavior

(32) What we do is usually a more effective witness than what we say. At least it makes what we say more effective. So St. Paul says to us:

Let everyone see that you are interested only in the highest ideals. (Rom 12:17)

The ideals which even the most degraded of men will reverence are love, joy, peace, patience, kindness, goodness, trustfulness, gentleness and self-control. By the power of the Holy Spirit these gifts are already ours if we use them for God's glory.

In the first encyclical letter on record we read this advice:

Always behave honorably among pagans so that they can see your good works for themselves. (1 Pt 2:12)

It is not always easy to behave honorably in a world where dishonorable behavior can be momentarily profitable. But this is the Christian duty. It is the Christian ideal if one is serious about bringing Jesus to others.

(33) For those who have responsibility for younger people — and we all have in one way or another if they see us at all — St. Paul gives this advice:

And in everything you do make yourself an example to them in your sincerity and earnestness and in keeping all that you say so wholesome that nobody can make objections to it. (Ti 2:7-8)

Even in our civic duty, we must be careful that we are not attacking authority just because it is authority. When our conscience tells us to do so we must do it, but with Christian restraint. On all other occasions more is asked from genuine Christians:

. . . to be obedient to the officials and representatives of government; to be ready to do good at every opportunity; not to go slandering other people or picking quarrels, but to be courteous and always polite to all kinds of people. (Ti 3:1-2)

(34) It is true that we must take a firm stand on many issues
        in our society whether it be war, racism, injustice,
pollution of the environment, etc., but the Christian stance is
to be "courteous and always polite to all kinds of people."
Aggression breeds only more aggression; courteous but firm
protest is more effective in the long run.

No better witness by behavior can be offered to the
unbelieving world than what is recommended by St. Paul
to the Christians of Thessalonica:

> *Make a point of living quiety, attending to your own*
> *business and earning your living . . . so that you are*
> *seen to be respectable by those outside the Church.*
> (1 Thes 4:11-12)

This is far from mere passivity; rather it is an active reminder to others that God lives in us and that we can offer
him to others as the only permanent solution for the many
ills of our modern society.

Witness by Concern and Detachment

(35) Although we have not here a lasting city, this world is
        our common home until the second coming of Christ;
this country, this town or city, this neighborhood. Like our
Lord and leader, we must be concerned about making this
a better world with more happiness for all. This may mean
less poverty. We should be in the forefront of any organization trying to alleviate poverty. And yet, we must know
that having enough to eat, drink, and to be clothed will
never in itself bring peace to the heart of man.

(36) While we work for more peace, less poverty, full racial
        justice or any other good cause, we are offering a
Christian witness — the witness of practical love — if our

work is manifestly inspired by the love of God. It is important that the means we use be godly too. Our attitude to all material things can be a powerful witness too. Do we appear to possess them or do they appear to possess us? Are we using material things such as money, clothes, food, housing, television or car as God wants?

(37) We have a right to possess whatever is necessary for our own and our family's needs. All others have the same right. It is wrong to take from another whether that other be a person, a company or the government.

But Jesus issued a clear warning against our being too attached to material things:

> *Watch and be on your guard against avarice of any kind, for a man's life is not made secure by what he owns, even when he has more than he needs.*
> (Lk 12:15)

Then he told them a parable.

(38)
> *There was once a rich man who, having had a good harvest from his land, thought to himself, "What am I to do? I have not enough room to store my crops." Then he said: "This is what I will do: I will pull down my barns and build bigger ones, and store all my grain and my goods in them, and I will say to my soul: My soul, you have plenty of good things laid by for many years to come; take things easy, eat, drink, have a good time." But God said to him, "Fool! This very night the demand will be made for your soul; and this hoard of yours, whose will it be then?" So it is when a man stores up treasure for himself in place of making*

himself rich in the sight of God. (Lk 12:16-21)

He had not stolen the treasure. It was his and he had worked to get it. Yet he was condemned. Why? Because he sought his full happiness in it and forgot God. He tried to make his heaven here below.

(39) It is easy to become a slave to material things. Jesus says:

No servant can be the slave of two masters; he will either hate the first and love the second, or treat the first with respect and the second with scorn. You cannot be the slave of both God and money. (Lk 16:13)

St. Paul says:

If any of the saints are in need, you must share with them. (Rom 12:13)

St. John says:

If a man who was rich enough in this world's goods saw that one of his brothers was in need, but closed his heart to him, how could the love of God be living in him? My children, our love is not to be just words or mere talk, but something real and active. (1 Jn 3:17-18)

God invites some to still greater detachment. To a rich young man who came to him Jesus said:

If you wish to be perfect, go and sell what you own and give the money to the poor. (Mt 19:21)

This is not a command to every Christian but an invitation to some. The response to this invitation is free. It usually implies living in close community with others where all things are held in common as the first Christians lived. God may be holding out this invitation to you.

Witness by Words

(40) People communicate mostly in words, but often our words are merely social noise or small talk. People crave for deeper communication at times especially in what are now called limit situations such as sickness, disaster or death. Serious subjects such as peace, war, social justice and the very structure of society itself are now becoming areas of active interest even in the local hotel and on the golf course. Faith too — this is not the same as "religion" — is fast becoming an area of concern to most thinking people today.

When we have established a genuine friendship with others and encouraged them to talk they will speak to us about areas of ultimate concern. Our witness in this case is outlined for us by St. Peter this way:

> *Reverence the Lord Christ in your hearts, and always have your answer ready for people who ask you for the reason for the hope that you all have. But give it with courtesy and respect and with a clear conscience.*
> (1 Pt 3:15-16)

(41) Notice that there is no question here of arguing about "religion"; this is generally useless. Neither is it a matter of defending the Church. It is neither arguing nor defending, *but explaining our personal faith* to a friend who asks us. The personal nature of this witness is stressed beautifully by St. Paul in this advice:

> *Be tactful with those who are not Christians and be sure*

you make the best use of your time with them. Talk
to them agreeably and with a flavor of wit, and try to fit
your answers to the needs of each one. (Col 4:5-6)

(42) Most of us may hesitate about doing this because we
feel that we lack a knowledge of theology or that we
cannot express ourselves well enough. Our faith should rid
us of these two fears. St. Paul says:

. . . in Christ, we speak as men of sincerity, as envoys
of God and in God's presence. (2 Cor 2:17)

The people we meet are far more impressed by our trans-
parent honesty than by the cleverness of our arguments.

We can always speak of our faith with great confidence
because Jesus speaks in us and through us.

It is not you who will be speaking.
The Spirit of your Father will be speaking in you.
(Mt 10:19-20)

It is his word not ours that evokes real faith in others.
Our voice is merely the channel through which God's word
becomes flesh when we speak it in the club, in the home,
on the golf course, on the beach or wherever we are.

Witness Through Our Missionaries

(43) Missionaries have left their homes or their country to
bring Jesus to people who have not heard of him. They
are lay people, sisters, brothers and priests who witness
with their very lives. They do this with our support. While
not everyone can go personally to another country as a
Christian missionary, we can all share in this important
aspect of Christian witness.

One of your children may be your gift to the missions and this is surely as close as you can get to being there yourself. Or it may be a brother or sister who is very dear to you or just a friend whose presence would mean so much to you. Or you may not know any of these genuine people personally. But no matter; as a parent, relative, friend, or aquaintance you are behind this person's witness by your love, your prayers and your offerings.

Or you may have made a similar contribution to the local church by parting with a son or daughter who became a priest in your diocese, a brother teaching in a parish school or a sister nursing the sick.

(44) Or you may be among the many generous people who support the Propagation of the Faith or the efforts of the missionary communities for the thousands of churchless people in our country.

Witness Within Your Family

Your first missionary thrust must take place within your own family. There by sharing, caring and, above all, by praying together you are truly apostolic and a good witness to Jesus. No activity outside your family will take the place of this one if you neglect it. Your first Christian duty is to help the members of your own household to God.

A Family Prayer:

Heavenly Father, you sanctified every family by sending your Son Jesus through the power of the Holy Spirit to be born and to grow up in a human family. Send your Holy Spirit into our home and family today so that each of us may learn how to love Jesus as our brother, and how to imitate him in faith and hope and love. Loving Father open our hearts so that we may see the many opportunities you give us to witness to Jesus every day. Take away our selfishness: give us a spirit of true poverty and detachment from material possessions so that others may come to Jesus through us.

Father give us a deep and genuine peace within our family so that all who know us may feel the joy and peace of Jesus in our home. Father teach us Christian hospitality so that our doors and our hearts may be open to all who come to us in need.

Holy Mary, mother of Jesus and our spiritual mother, may we grow daily stronger in your spirit of faith and love.

POINTS FOR DISCUSSION

1. What are some practical implications for Christians of the claim that Jesus wants his message to continue to be heard through us?

2. List some reasons why every Christian has an obligation to witness for Jesus.

3. Recall and discuss some particular cases where you felt true Christian witness was given either by yourself or another Christian.

4. List and discuss some examples of a strong stand on moral and social issues which could be seen as genuine Christian witness.

REVIEW

1. The gospel must first be experienced as good news before it is passed on.   T   F

2. Jesus came on earth to make God's name and God's love known.   T   F

3. A Christian continues to make God's name and love known.   T   F

4. A Christian is a witness to, a sign of, an experience of God's love to others.   T   F

5. All men will love and listen to our witness of God's love.   T   F

6. A Christian is a witness to the death of Jesus.   T   F

7. A Christian is a witness to the resurrection which verified Jesus' claim to have come from God.   T   F

8. A Christian's primary work is to explain the teaching of the Church to others.   T   F

9. A Christian community which does not look outwards is not fully Christian.   T   F

10. It is only bishops and priests who must make disciples of others. T F

11. We can silence Jesus today by our own silence. T F

12. It is not my business to speak of Jesus to others. T F

13. Most of us have not the power to preach to others. T F

14. As Christians we have the power to "bear fruit in plenty." T F

15. Our best witness is to show others how we love those around us. T F

16. Accepting others who have views different from our own in the Church is an important witness today. T F

17. The first Christians had no difficulties in tolerating one another. T F

18. Worship is an important witness in God's plan. T F

19. Christian behavior must appear different from that of pagans. T F

20. A firm stand on social issues can be
    an important Christian witness.   T   F

21. How we are attached to material
    things and how we use them is not
    important.   T   F

22. Arguing about our religion and
    defending it is more effective than
    explaining our personal faith.   T   F

23. The first witness of a Christian must
    be within his or her own family.   T   F

Chapter 9

SURE HOPE OF GLORY

(1)   As Christians we are pilgrims traveling toward "the glory as yet unrevealed, which is waiting for us" (Rom 8:18). When St. Paul was on trial before the entire Jewish court, we read that he "looked steadily" at them and said:

It is for our hope in the resurrection of the dead that I am on trial. (Acts 23:6)

In these few words — because he had to be brief — he summarized the Christianity he preached. He was prepared to face prison or death on this central issue, *his personal hope of one day sharing the resurrection of Jesus.*

(2)   When he wrote to the Christians at Colossae to encourage them in their struggles, he reminded them that they could hope to "join the saints and with them inherit the light one day." This hope, he assured them, would give them power to "bear anything joyfully":

You will have in you the strength, based on his own glorious power, never to give in, but to bear anything joyfully, thanking the Father who has made it possible for you to join the saints and with them inherit the light. (Col 1:11-12)

(3)   This faith in the resurrection of Jesus and this hope in
our own resurrection is central to the Christian life.

The Christian Life Is a Journey

(4)   The life we lead as Christians is a journey — a journey
to the vision of God. All journeys call for endurance
and effort; a journey always entails the determination to
keep going. In every journey there is a tension between the
present (the traveling) and the future (the arrival). The
traveler is always in a place which is not his home; he is
leaving place after place in order to get to the place which
he has not reached. This implies a constant effort and a
continual determination to keep moving even when it is
not easy.

(5)   This determination to keep going needs something else
to keep it alive. It needs a conviction that the goal at
the end of the journey can be attained; it needs a real hope
that getting there is possible. If for a moment the traveler
thinks he will not get there or that the place he plans to
reach is not really accessible, he will lose hope and give up.

Hope then is the flame in the heart of man which gives
a feeling of power to his feet; it is the strength within his
spirit which gives muscle to his tired legs; it is the drive
within him which gives him the determination to keep going.
It is most of all the ability to see the future to come as if
it were already present and in the strength of this to struggle
on. Hope sees victory before the victory is enjoyed. As we
say at Mass:

We hope to enjoy forever the vision of your glory.
(Eucharistic Prayer 3)

Strength for the Journey

(6) The Christian journey on which we travel calls for drive, for determination and for power. It is Christian hope which gives this power — the hope of eternal glory, as St. Paul writing from prison said:

> *The mystery is Christ among you, your hope of glory . . . . It is for this that I struggle wearily on, helped only by his power driving me irresistibly.* (Col 1:27-9)

We must pray for an understanding of Christian hope, and an awareness that it is already given to us at baptism. It will then give us what it gave Paul — *a certainty which is not deceptive* as well as the joy which never fails. Let us first look prayerfully at the journey of God's people, then at the journey of God's Son and finally at our own journey.

The Journey of God's People

(7) When a desert nomad left his tribe, it meant almost certain death. To wander alone left one open to attack from others, to possible starvation and to loneliness, which is hardest of all. Yet this is what God asked Abraham to do.

> *Leave your country, your family and your father's house, for the land I will show you.* (Gen 12:1)

Humanly speaking, it was unwise to a remarkable degree. It was a journey to almost certain disaster and to possible death. But we know that Abraham and his wife set out.

(8) It was a long and laborious journey, taking 40 years. Like you or I on a difficult journey, these people too needed determination and strength to keep going; they needed the power which comes only from a sure hope that

their destination was within their reach, that victory was possible.

(9)   Their strength for the struggle came from hope in
      God's promise:

*I will make you a great nation; I will bless you and make
your name so famous that it will be used as a blessing.
I will bless those who bless you; I will curse those who
slight you. All the tribes of the earth shall bless
themselves by you.* (Gen 12:2-3)

This word of God was the source of their hope and so of their determination to step out on what looked like an imprudent journey and to keep going even when humanly speaking it looked hopeless to continue.

(10) When Moses was told by God to go to Pharaoh and
      bring the sons of Israel out of Egypt, he asked, "Who
am I to do this?" God's reply was simple: "I shall be with you." In other words, Moses was reminded that his hope of success was not in himself, but in the promised presence of God. When the Israelites forgot this promise and feared the Egyptians pursuing them, Moses built up their hope:

*Have no fear! Stand firm, and you will see what Yahweh
will do to save you today . . . . Yahweh will do the
fighting for you: you have only to keep still.*
(Ex 14:13-14)

(11) It was a journey from slavery to freedom but this was
      not apparent to the travelers during most of the jour-
ney and at one time they asked:

Is Yahweh with us, or not?

(12) But God did honor the promise which he had made when he said:

I will adopt you as my people, and I will be your God.
(Ex 6:7)

In the strength of this promise alone they reached the promised land because they continued to hope.

(13) This pilgrimage of the people of God in the Old Testament is a *pattern event* for our own Christian lives to strengthen our journey to God. A promise sustained their hope; a promise sustains ours.

The Journey of God's Son

(14) Jesus too needed hope on his earthly journey. We know that he was like us in everything except sin; he was fully human:

He emptied himself to assume the condition of a slave, and became as men are. (Phil 2:7)

(15) Before him throughout his life was the human fear of the death which he knew he would undergo. There was also the apparent meaninglessness of this death from a human point of view. In the garden of Gethsemani, as his whole emotional life became deeply upset to the point of "his sweat falling to the ground like great drops of blood," he prayed:

My Father, if it is possible, let this cup pass me by . . . .
(Mt 26:39)

(16) But this moment of extreme tension is but the pinnacle point of a life during which he had undergone all the pressures of a pilgrimage like our own in every way. He

has some success and much apparent failure from the first temptations which he underwent in the desert right up to the final one in the garden of Gethsemani. Some men had believed him, some had not, some had followed him and some had failed him.

(17) Yet, he never lost the certain hope that his Father would bring his body from the tomb in a glorious resurrection. This was his sustaining certainty. And it was for this reason that even as he walked with his disciples down into the Cedron valley and to death, that he could say:

I have told you this so that my own joy may be in you and your joy be complete. (Jn 15:11)

and

Peace I bequeath to you, my own peace I give you, a peace the world cannot give, this is my gift to you. Do not let your hearts be troubled or afraid. You have heard me say: "I am going away, and shall return."
(Jn 14:27-28)

(18) Hope seems to leave us most of all when we are deserted by friends in a time of need. But Jesus had a deeper hope than human friendship gives. He had the certainty that his Father was with him:

Listen; the time will come—in fact it has come already —when you will be scattered, each going his own way and leaving me alone. Yet, I am not alone, because the Father is with me. (Jn 16:32)

(19) And he continues with this message of hope and victory, offering to share it with the very men who would soon desert him for a time:

*I have told you all this so that you may find peace in
me. In the world you will have trouble, but be brave;
I have conquered the world.* (Jn 16:33)

In another place he said the same thing in different words:

*In a short time you will no longer see me, and then a
short time later and you will see me again . . . you
are sad now, but I shall see you again, and your hearts
will be full of joy, and that joy no one shall take from
you.* (Jn 16:16, 22)

(20) This is how Jesus experienced his journey; this is what
his pilgrimage meant to him. It was a victory in the
future, but a victory he was so sure of that in a way it
was already present — "I shall return" (Jn 14:3).

Our Journey Is His

(21) The life of Jesus too is a *pattern event* of our lives. It
was a journey in hope of what was to come; it was
based on a certainty that God's promises were true; it was
sustained by the foreseen resurrection in the power of God.
It is hope like this — rather, it is exactly the same hope, the
hope of Jesus himself living in us by his Holy Spirit —
which gives power and push, drive and direction to your life
and mine if we really believe and step out on that faith.
This is exactly what he promised us — his joy, his peace,
his hope, his victory:

*So that my own joy may be in you . . . .
My own peace I give you . . . .
Be brave, I have conquered the world.
I shall see you again and your hearts will be full of joy,
and that joy no one shall take from you.*

A Journey in Hope

> . . . *We look for the resurrection of the dead, and the*
> *life of the world to come.* (Creed)

(22) These words of the Creed express the faith of the
Church. Those who believe this are members of the
Church of God. When the first leaders in the Church were
about to choose a man to take the place of Judas (he had
lost hope in the promised resurrection of Jesus) they stated
that they wanted someone who:

> *Can act with us as a witness to his resurrection.* (Acts
> 1:22)

(23) And when Paul spoke to the learned men of Athens,
they listened to him until he reached the core of the
Christian message:

> *Even a few Epicurean and Stoic philosophers argued*
> *with him. Some said, "Does this parrot know what he's*
> *talking about?" And because he was preaching about*
> *Jesus and the resurrection, others said, "he sounds like*
> *a propagandist for some outlandish gods."* (Acts 17:18)

Despite the fact that he did not have success with them,
Paul kept preaching the central hope of the Christian
Church. When he was on trial even before the Roman
governor, Felix, he said:

> *. . . there will be a resurrection of good men and bad*
> *men alike.* (Acts 24:15)

(24) This is still the hope which sustains the people of God
on their journey between Pentecost and the final coming of Jesus. In fact, it is a firm hope in this which makes
us Christians. This certain hope in our own resurrection

because of the resurrection of Jesus, is the first fruits of the faith we profess as outlined in an earlier chapter. We are the pilgrim people of God like his pilgrim people of the Old Testament. When the Church received the Spirit of God at Pentecost it received a *promise,* a *covenant,* a *sign* assuring it of a future share in the resurrection of its Lord.

(25) We, the new people of God, are *wayfarers to resurrection.* Because, like Jesus, we have to struggle against the forces of Satan and to draw other men into our community, we live in constant tension, in continual crisis. This is in the sense that every journey is tension, crisis, effort and struggle. And, as in every journey, it is only an abiding hope in the certainty of eventual homecoming which sustains us. The Church then is a community of pilgrims who:

> *Wait in joyful hope for the coming of our Savior, Jesus Christ.* (Communion Rite)

It is important to tell God this often and to pray for a fuller hope in what we look forward to.

A Journey That Will End

(26) Our journey as Christians, our pilgrimage as members of the people of God begins at baptism and is completed at death. It is a lived-out testimony to our faith in Jesus' resurrection and to hope in our own.

> *We too believe and therefore we too speak, knowing that he who raised the Lord Jesus to life will raise us with Jesus in our turn and put us by his side.*
> (2 Cor 4:13)

(27) The actual physical resurrection of Jesus is the basis of

Christian hope. Our faith and our hope which follows
from this faith rest on the resurrection and final victory of
Jesus. From this we gain our courage and our immovable
security.

> *That is why there is no weakening on our part, and
> instead, though this outer man of ours may be falling
> into decay, the inner man is renewed day by day. Yes,
> the troubles which are soon over, though they weigh
> little, train us for the carrying of a weight of eternal
> glory which is out of all proportion to them. And so we
> have no eyes for things that are visible; for visible
> things last only for a time, and the invisible things are
> eternal. (2 Cor 4:16-18)*

(28) Thus the Christian's view of life is very different from
that of those who have no faith. We know that food is
nourishing, that sex is enjoyable, that television can be
entertaining, that carpets are comfortable and that surfing
is fun. However,

> *there is no eternal city for us in this life but we look
> for one in the life to come. (Heb 13:14)*

Do we really believe this? Do we really believe that heaven
can never be found here?

A Prayer:

(29)

> *O God my Father in heaven, I believe that you love
> me. I believe that you created me to share your
> love forever in heaven. I rely completely on your
> mercy and love. I am truly sorry for having ever
> turned away from you by sin. Wash away all my sins
> by the blood of Jesus. I sincerely hope to be happy
> with you forever in heaven.*

Death Was Victory for Jesus

(30) One day when some Greek visitors to Jerusalem came
to speak with Jesus, he referred to his coming death
but identified it with his final victory:

> *Now the hour has come for the Son of Man to be
> glorified. But I tell you most solemnly, unless a wheat
> grain falls on the ground and dies, it remains only a
> single grain; but if it dies, it yields a rich harvest.*
> (Jn 12:23-24)

And in his glorious resurrection, the Father would be
glorified too. We read:

> *What shall I say: Father, save me from this hour?
> But it was for this very reason that I have come to this
> hour. Father, glorify your name!* (Jn 12:27-28)

A voice came from heaven:

> *I have glorified it, and will glorify it again.* (Jn 12:28)

Here we have a public divine sanctioning of Jesus' coming
death as part of his final victory and of the Father's glory.

We Share in the Victory of Jesus

> *But when Christ is revealed—and he is your life—
> you too will be revealed in all your glory with him.*
> (Col 3:4)

(31) What a wonderful assurance Paul offers every Christian — a share in the final glory of Jesus. And this is
because we are the brothers and sisters of Jesus. We are
now privileged, by the almost unbelievable goodness of
God, to claim God our Father, and to know that all he has

220 RENEWAL OF FAITH

is ours and will one day be enjoyed if we persevere in faith.

The Father said, "My son, ... all I have is yours."
(Lk 15:31)

(32) No wonder then that St. John frequently reminds us
of the basis of our Christian hope:

*Think of the love that the Father has lavished on us, by
letting us be called God's children; and that is what we
are . . . . My dear people, we are already the children of
God but what we are to be in the future has not yet
been revealed; all we know is, that when it is revealed
we shall be like him because we shall see him as he
really is.* (1 Jn 3:1-2)

(33) Then St. Paul tells us:

*And if we are children we are heirs as well: heirs of God
and coheirs with Christ, sharing his suffering so as to
share his glory.* (Rom 8:17)

(34) Heaven and the vision of God are already ours by
hope.

*And this hope is not deceptive, because the love of
God has already been poured into our hearts by the
Holy Spirit which has been given us.* (Rom 5:5)

We Hope But We Are Sure

(35) Usually when we hope, we are not certain of results.
If we hope that our team will win, or that a movie will
be good or that the surf will be pleasant, we are saying that
we would like it that way and that we think it might be so.

But Christian hope is much more than this; it is certain even though the goal is not yet fully experienced. In most cases human hope depends on something we cannot be entirely sure of, or on our own efforts which may or may not be good enough. But our Christian hope does not depend on something which we are unsure of, and certainly not on our own efforts. Many people, for instance, put their hope in money and material things, but Timothy was told by St. Paul:

Warn those who are rich in this world's goods . . . not to set their hope on money which is untrustworthy, but on God who, out of his riches, gives us all that we need for our happiness. (1 Tm 6:17)

(36) This is a prayer which Christians should offer for one another:

May our Lord Jesus Christ himself, and God our Father who has given us his love and, through his grace, such inexhaustible comfort and such sure hope, comfort you and strengthen you in everything good that you do and say. (2 Thes 2:16-17)

(37) So, it is in God's word and his truthfulness that we hope, because we are:

. . . those whom God has chosen to faith and to the knowledge of the truth that leads to true religion; and to give them the hope of the eternal life that was promised so long ago by God. He does not lie. . . . (Ti 1:1-3)

Let us keep firm in the hope we profess, because the one who made the promise is faithful. (Heb 10:23)

*. . . it was impossible for God to be lying, and so that
we, now we have found safety, should have a strong
encouragement to take firm grip on the hope that is
held out to us. Here we have an anchor for our soul,
as sure as it is firm, and reaching right through beyond
the veil where Jesus has entered before us and on our
behalf . . . .* (Heb 6:18-20)

(38) Our hope then has the firmest possible basis:

Christ Jesus, our hope. (1 Tm 1:1)

The mystery is Christ among you, your hope of glory."
(Col 1:26)

And so,

*We are filled with joyful trust in God through our Lord
Jesus Christ through whom we have already gained
our reconciliation.* (Rom 5:11)

Do you experience this joyful trust in your life? Are you
really sure that Jesus is "your hope of glory"?

Hope Is Not Vision

(39) Christian hope is different from every other kind of
hope; it is sure because it is founded on a promise
made by someone who has power to carry it out and who
cannot lie. It can never be mistaken. But it is still hope;
it is not yet a homecoming.

*We must be content to hope that we shall be saved —
our salvation is not in sight, we should not have to be
hoping for it if it were — but I say, we must hope to
be saved since we are not saved yet — it is something we must wait for with patience.* (Rom 8:24-25)

(40) At each Mass as a community "looking forward to his
    coming in glory, we offer you (the Father) his body
and blood" and thus celebrate a certainty that is to come,
and say:

> *Christ has died, Christ has risen, Christ will come
> again.*

In union with Jesus present on the altar, we say that:

> *We hope to enjoy forever, the vision of your (the
> Father's) glory through Christ our Lord, from whom
> all good things come.* (Eucharistic Prayer 3)

and we also say in another Eucharistic Prayer:

> *Then in your kingdom, freed from the corruption of
> sin and death, we shall sing your glory with every
> creature through Christ our Lord, through whom you
> give us everything that is good.*

So, "having this hope we can be quite confident" (2 Cor
3:12). That is why we use the word "celebration" in con-
nection with Mass. We are celebrating a victory already
won even if not yet fully experienced.

Hope Is God's Gift

(41) But as with faith, so also hope is a *gift* flowing from,
    and intimately dependent on, our faith in the resurrec-
tion of Jesus.

> *God, who raised the Lord from the dead, will by his
> power raise us up too.* (1 Cor 6:14)

> *Surely we may count on being saved by the life of his
> Son?* (Rom 5:10)

(42) It is only on the life, death and resurrection of Jesus that we can hope. We should pray for one another and remind one another that:

Thanks be to God who . . . makes us, in Christ, partners in his triumph, and through us is spreading the knowledge of himself, like a sweet smell, everywhere. (2 Cor 2:14)

(43) So then, instead of ever claiming this hope as something we can generate by ourselves or as something we have earned, we ought to recall St. Paul's exhortation to the Corinthians:

Remember it is God himself who assures us all, and you, of our standing in Christ, and has anointed us, marking us with his seal and giving us the pledge, the Spirit, that we carry in our hearts. (2 Cor 1:21-22)

Hope and Suffering

(44) We live in an age which seems to have more doubt and insecurity and suffering than earlier ages. And each of us has his and her own share of personal sufferings. It may be loneliness, doubt, economic insecurity, an illness, or a broken marriage. Even if we were not Christians, these things would be part of life and we would have to meet them with one attitude or another. We know, of course, that by our faith God will often cure illnesses and remove doubts, but he does not free us from all sufferings. Just as Jesus' resurrection was closely connected with his sufferings, so too are the sufferings of the Christian. In fact, his sufferings and ours are identified if we live a life of faith and hope. We share his sufferings so as to share his glory, as St. Paul assures us (cf. Rom 8:17).

(45) Faith and hope assure us that God is faithful in his
     love even when he permits suffering and so St. Peter
reminds us:

> *So even those whom God allows to suffer must trust*
> *themselves to the constancy of the creator and go on*
> *doing good.* (1 Pt 4:19)

(46) If ever we find ourselves losing hope in God's abiding
     love, it will help us to recall a beautiful passage about
suffering from the letter to the Hebrews.

> *Have you forgotten that encouraging text in which*
> *you are addressed as sons? My sons, when the Lord*
> *corrects you, do not treat it lightly; but do not get*
> *discouraged when he reprimands you. For the Lord*
> *trains the ones that he loves and punishes all those*
> *that he acknowledges as his sons. Suffering is part*
> *of your training. God is treating you as his sons. Has*
> *there ever been any son whose Father did not train*
> *him?* (Heb 12:5-7)

(47) But this does not mean we should not pray for a release
     in part or in whole from our emotional or mental suf-
ferings. In fact, prayer is the response of the hope-filled
Christian in face of suffering.

> *Do not give up if trials come; and keep on praying.*
> (Rom 12:12)

> *And indeed everything that was written long ago in*
> *the scriptures was meant to teach us something about*
> *hope from the examples scripture gives us of how*
> *people who did not give up were helped by God.*
> (Rom 15:4)

(48) St. Paul sums up the Christian attitude to suffering:

> *All I want is to know Christ and the power of his resur-*
> *rection and to share his sufferings by reproducing the*
> *pattern of his death.* (Phil 3:10)

(49) Finally, suffering reminds us that we are only on a
       journey, that final happiness is not here. So our suffer-
ings can increase hope in us.

> *These sufferings bring patience, as we know, and*
> *patience brings perseverance, and perseverance*
> *brings hope, and this hope is not deceptive, because*
> *the love of God has been poured into our hearts by*
> *the Holy Spirit which has been given to us.* (Rom 5:4-5)

A Christian Looks at Death

(50) In the Preface of the Mass which is celebrated at
       Catholic funerals the priest prays:

> *Father, all powerful and ever-living God, we do*
> *well always and everywhere to give you thanks through*
> *Jesus Christ our Lord. In him, who rose from the*
> *dead, our hope of resurrection dawned. The sadness*
> *of death gives way to the bright promise of immortali-*
> *ty. Lord, for your faithful people life is changed, not*
> *ended. When the body of our earthly dwelling lies in*
> *death we gain an everlasting dwelling in heaven. . . .*

When a friend dies, let us recall this and think of our own
death as final victory too.

(51) St. Paul looked at life as a *tent dwelling* and at death as *homecoming.*

For we know that when the tent that we live in on earth is folded up, there is a house built by God for us, an everlasting home not made by human hands, in the heavens. In this present state, it is true, we groan as we wait with longing to put on our heavenly home over the other . . . . This is the purpose for which God made us, and he has given us a pledge of the Spirit.

We are always full of confidence, then, when we remember that to live in the body means to be exiled from the Lord, going as we do by faith and not by sight — we are full of confidence, I say, and actually want to be exiled from the body and make our home with the Lord. (2 Cor 5:1-9)

This is the Christian attitude to death; it can be ours if we pray. Christian hope enables us to think like this about our death.

Christian Hope Is an Experience

(52) Christian hope makes a real difference here and now. Hope is an experience of *joy* and *peace:*

May the God of hope bring you such joy and peace in your faith that the power of the Holy Spirit will remove all bounds to hope. (Rom 15:13)

(53) Hope is an experience of *comfort* and *strength:*

May our Lord Jesus Christ himself, and God our Father who has given us his love and, through his grace, such inexhaustible comfort and such sure hope, com-

fort you and strengthen you in everything good that you do or say. (2 Thes 2:16-17)

(54) Hope is an experience of *confidence:*

And we are his house, as long as we cling to our hope with the confidence that we glory in. (Heb 3:6)

(55) Hope is an experience of *cheerfulness:*

If you have hope, this will make you cheerful. (Rom 12:12)

(56) Hope is an experience of *perseverance:*

We always mention you in our prayers and thank God for you all and constantly remember how you have . . . persevered through hope in our Lord Jesus Christ. (1 Thes 1:3)

(57) Hope is an experience of *victory:*

It is by faith and through Jesus that we have entered this state of grace in which we can boast about looking forward to God's glory. (Rom 5:2)

(58) Do we experience these in our own lives? Perhaps we lack joy or peace, or feel that we are without comfort, confidence or strength. Could it be that at times we feel we won't persevere and are full of fears? Christian hope drives out doubts and fears because Christian hope gives joy, peace, comfort, strength, confidence, cheerfulness, perseverance, a reason to boast and an untroubled heart.

A Joy So Glorious

(59) We cannot summarize this chapter and the entire book
    better than in the words of God himself when through
Peter he spoke to his new people.

It is something which we should pray about very slowly
and very often. Every word is precious and full of meaning for us who believe:

(60)

Blessed be God the Father of our Lord Jesus Christ,
who in his great mercy has given us a new birth as
his sons, by raising Jesus Christ from the dead, so that
we have a sure hope and the promise of an inheritance
that can never be spoilt or soiled or fade away, be-
cause it is being kept for you in the heavens. Through
your faith, God's power will guard you until the salva-
tion which has been prepared is revealed at the end
of time. This is a cause of great joy for you, even
though you may for a short time have to bear being
plagued by all sorts of trials; so that, when Jesus
Christ is revealed, your faith will have been tested and
proved like gold — only it is more precious than gold,
which is corruptible even though it bears testing by
fire — and, then you will have praise and glory and
honor. You did not see him, yet you love him; and still
without seeing him you are already filled with a joy
so glorious that it cannot be described, because you
believe; you are sure of the end to which your faith
looks forward, that is, the salvation of your souls.
(1 Pt 1:3-9)

POINTS FOR DISCUSSION

1. Why do we say that the life of a Christian is a journey in hope based on the resurrection of Jesus?

2. Why do we say that the life of Jesus is a *pattern event* for the life of every Christian?

3. Discuss the statement, "Faith is for now, hope is for the future."

4. How does the virtue of hope give the Christian power to accept suffering with patience? How does it help those who are incurably ill?

REVIEW

1. A Christian lives in sure hope of
    resurrection.   T   F

2. Hope can give us the power to bear
    anything joyfully.   T   F

3. Hope gives drive and determination to
    keep going if we seek it.   T   F

4. The journey of the first chosen people
    is a pattern event for our journey.   T   F

5. Jesus did not need hope for his earthly
    journey.   T   F

6. We can share in Christ's already-won
    victory over the world by Christian hope.   T   F

7. The Christian life is a journey in hope.   T   F

8. God's promise is the source of our hope.   T   F

9. The Christian view of life is different
    from all others because of hope.   T   F

10. Jesus' death was the moment of his
    failure because men rejected him.   T   F

11. We share in the victory of Jesus by
    Christian hope.   T   F

12. Heaven and the vision of God are
    already ours by hope.   T   F

13. Christian hope is like all hope; it is
    not sure.   T   F

14. Hope is the same thing as seeing God
    face to face.   T   F

15. Because hope is not vision it cannot be
    a source of joy.   T   F

16. Hope is a gift from God given when
    we ask and act on it.   T   F

17. Suffering tests hope.   T   F

18. Because of Christian hope we should
    never ask for the removal of suffering. T   F

19. All suffering for a Christian is a share
    in the suffering of Christ.   T   F

20. For the Christian, life is a tent
    dwelling and death a homecoming.   T   F

21. Hope cannot be experienced in this
    life.   T   F

22. Hope is a substitute for comfort and
    strength.   T   F

23. Christian hope can now give us a joy
    so glorious that it cannot be described. T   F

Appendix

DIRECTIONS FOR GROUP USE

The material in this book can be used by both individuals and groups. Its value, however, both spiritually and educationally, is normally enhanced when studied in groups. Members of the group grow together in faith and love:

(a) by hearing God's word,
(b) by sharing their experience of it,
(c) by encouraging each other to live it,
(d) by praying together.

To Start a Group

Any Catholic should be able to start a group. A person who has already studied the book himself is particularly well suited to do so. Starting a group is a splendid act of Christian witness.

Find a few friends who are willing to discuss the book with you. Any number from four to about ten is suitable for a small private group. Decide on a time and a place where you can all meet one night a week for ten weeks.

Go to a different location each week if you wish, e.g., one
another's homes.

The Preliminary Meeting

The first meeting will be devoted to general preparation.
Appoint someone other than the leader to be treasurer and
timekeeper. A timekeeper is more important than may
appear. If your group is to be a success you need a definite time for starting and, even more important, a definite
time for finishing. Your timekeeper's first duty is to
say "time to start" and "time to finish," and insist upon it.
Let the group decide at this preliminary meeting how long
the weekly meeting ought to take. We recommend an hour
and a half with perhaps an extra ten minutes for coffee
when you finish. The treasurer will take responsibility for
collecting the cost of the books.

The leader should explain that it is essential that everyone should study the contents of the chapters fully at home
before the meetings. The particular chapter is background
reading for the weekly meeting at which it will be prayed
about, discussed and assimilated, but not read. The review
at the end of the chapter should also be filled in at home.

Regular Weekly Meeting

If you have not had the opportunity of leading a group
the following six steps will help you. The times suggested
for each step are suitable for a group of up to about ten
members.

  (1) Opening Prayers   (5 minutes)
  (2) God's Personal Message (10 minutes)
  (3) The Review   (40 minutes)

(4) The Discussion Points   (20 minutes)
(5) Personal Witness   (10 minutes)
(6) Closing Prayers   (5 minutes)

(1) Opening Prayers

Every meeting ought to begin with shared prayer. Try to make this prayer spontaneous. Each one might make a short prayer ending with "Lord hear us," as we do in the Prayer of the Faithful at Mass. Some may find this difficult at first, but if persevered in, it has a very great liberating and unifying effect on the group.

(2) God's Personal Message

Each member of the group tells the others in a few words (about one minute) what he feels is the main thing God said to him through the chapter as he studied it. There is no discussion at this point; you simply say what you feel and the others listen and ponder it.

(3) The Review

The leader reads out the statements on the review one by one. The others in turn express an opinion on the statement (*saying whether it is true or false*) and give a reason for the opinion expressed. The leader goes on to the next statement, and so on to the end. An average of only one to two minutes is spent on each statement. Some points are more fruitful for dialogue than others. Be free to pass quickly over some and to dwell on others. The leader can use the guide to the reviews in the back of the book to help him with this section of the meeting.

(4) The Discussion Points

These are taken one at a time and each member candidly expresses what he or she has to say about them. Some groups may like to add an extra half hour to the weekly meeting and use it here. Small groups may save time on other steps and add it on here. Some may even like to devote two meetings to each chapter.

(5) Personal Witness

Fifteen minutes before closing time the timekeeper reminds the group it is time for the *personal witness*. This means that each one takes about one minute to state simply what he or she as a Christian feels called upon to do as a result of the contents of the chapter and the prayer and discussion that have followed from it. It may sometimes be simply a request for prayer support from the others for some special effort; or it may be an acknowledgment of a new opportunity discovered for Christian witness; or maybe a humble statement of a resolution.

(6) Closing Prayers

This ought to be quite spontaneous and simple and from the heart, each one in turn speaking a few words to God in deep humility and with faith in the great power of prayer. Some may like to sing a hymn together.

KEY TO REVIEW QUESTIONS

Quest. No.	Chapter 1 Ans. Par.	Chapter 2 Ans. Par.	Chapter 3 Ans. Par.
1	T. 1	F. 1	F. 4
2	T. 2	T. 3	T. 3, 4
3	F. 3	F. 6	T. 5, 6
4	F. 4	T. 5	T. 7
5	F. 6, 7	F. 1	F. 8
6	T. 6	F. 8	T. 9
7	F. 8	F. 13	F. 10
8	F. 9	F. 12	T. 11
9	F. 9	F. 12	T. 12, 13
10	T. 9	T. 13, 15	F. 17
11	F. 11	F. 16	T. 16
12	F. 17	T. 17	T. 19
13	F. 14	F. 18	F. 26
14	T. 16	F. 20	T. 23
15	T. 18	T. 20	T. 25
16	T. 21	F. 21, 22	T. 29
17	T. 24	T. 23	T. 31, 32
18	F. 24, 25	T. 26	T. 33
19	T. 23	T. 26	T. 34
20	F. 29	F. 31	T. 27
21	F. 32, 33	F. 33	T. 45, 46
22	T. 38, 39	T. 38	F. 48
23	F. 43	T. 40	F. 48
24	—	F. 43	T. 48
25	—	—	T. 52

Quest.	Chapter 4		Chapter 5		Chapter 6	
No.	Ans. Par.		Ans. Par.		Ans. Par.	
1	T.	2	F.	1	T.	1–4
2	T.	4	T.	2	T.	8
3	F.	6	T.	4	F.	5, 7
4	T.	8	T.	6	F.	10
5	T.	9, 15	F.	7	T.	11–13
6	T.	14	F.	8	F.	14, 15
7	F.	17	T.	10	F.	18
8	F.	19	F.	15	T.	22
9	F.	21	T.	17	T.	25
10	T.	26	F.	19	F.	29
11	T.	30, 33	T.	20	T.	31
12	T.	39, 40	T.	22	F.	33–38
13	F.	41, 42	T.	26	T.	35
14	T.	43	F.	27	F.	36
15	F.	48	F.	28	T.	39
16	F.	48	T.	29	T.	40, 41
17	T.	49	F.	30	F.	43
18	T.	51	F.	32	T.	45
19	T.	54	F.	33	F.	45
20	T.	55	T.	34	F.	49
21	T.	57	T.	37	T.	55
22	T.	60	F.	39	T.	59
23	F.	62	T.	41	T.	63
24	—		—		—	
25	—		—		—	

Quest.	Chapter 7	Chapter 8	Chapter 9
No.	Ans. Par.	Ans. Par.	Ans. Par.
1	T. 2	T. 1	T. 1
2	T. 5	T. 2	T. 2
3	T. 6, 11	T. 3	T. 1, 6, 8
4	F. 12	T. 6	T. 13
5	T. 13	F. 7	F. 14, 20
6	T. 15	F. 9	T. 18
7	T. 18	T. 9	T. 25
8	T. 19, 21	F. 11	T. 24
9	T. 23	T. 13	T. 28
10	T. 24	F. 14	F. 29
11	T. 27	T. 16	T. 32
12	F. 28	F. 17	T. 34
13	T. 31	F. 18, 21, 22	F. 35
14	F. 34	T. 22	F. 39
15	T. 34	T. 23, 25	F. 38
16	F. 40	T. 26	T. 42, 43
17	F. 39	F. 27	T. 44
18	T. 41	T. 30	F. 47
19	F. 41	T. 32, 34	T. 48
20	T. 44, 48	T. 34	T. 51
21	T. 52	F. 35, 39	F. 52, 57
22	T. 52	F. 41	F. 53
23	T. 61, 67	T. 45	T. 60
24	—	—	—
25	—	—	—

Pg 84 - God's love living in us
Pg 89-90 loving sacrifice of praise
93 power { to do + to avoid
freedom {
95 - a gift accepted